I0749179

GULSIFAT SHAKHIDI

# LORD OF DARKNESS

Published by Hertfordshire Press Ltd © 2024
e-mail: publisher@hertfordshirepress.com
www.hertfordshirepress.com

GULSIFAT SHAKHIDI

LORD OF DARKNESS

*English - Gift edition*

Translators - Timur Akhmedjanov, John Farndon

Editor - Francesca Mepham

Design - Alexandra Rey

---



*British Library Catalogue in Publication Data*
*A catalogue record for this book is available from the British Library*
*Library of Congress in Publication Data*
*A catalogue record for this book has been requested*

**ISBN: 978-1-913356-73-6**

# Contents

# Fröm the Authör

I have always tried to avoid using negative imagery in the titles of my books, avoiding names and expressions that evoke fear or anxiety. But this time I couldn't resist, and there is a good reason for that. A terrible and tragic page has opened in the history of my beloved Tajikistan, a country of kind, creative, hardworking and wonderful people. Many women, unable to cope with domestic violence, are making a desperate last choice - suicide. There were cases like these in Soviet times, but they were all kept silent and not particularly publicized.

Now they write about everything. The worst thing is that these women not only kill themselves, but also their young children. I decided to find out the truth in publications on different sites. I read and listened, with tears in my eyes, to the voices of many desperate women who were saved from death. I mentally entered an argument with them, trying to convince them to be strong. I wanted to make mothers understand, because we are responsible before God for all our actions.

But gradually I realized that in a society where patriarchy still reigns, where men have their own law and their own truth, it sometimes becomes impossible to solve family problems. Our Tajikistan has scaled economic heights - it has "jumped," as Sovietologists like to say, “from feudalism to socialism,” but in terms of human thinking, it has remained largely dormant.

So, I decided to write a work of art on this topic. Maybe, after reading my new story, women will not look for a way out through suicide, and men will not drive them to despair...

There is a good proverb in the Tajik language: ‘Khonasheri Maydon-garib,’ meaning; ‘At home - a lion, and outside, a lamb.’ It is very suitable for those who behave like usurpers in the family, but in public they seem intelligent, kind, well-mannered and educated. Therefore, people rarely believe women who are victims of violence.

This all comes from ignorance. Many people know neither the Divine Scripture nor the laws of society, and instead live by traditions and rules ‘written’ to please men and heads of family clans over the ages. It’s as if it’s not even the 20th century! Girls in villages are not allowed to study, and they are given away in marriage when they are young, sometimes to be ‘torn to pieces’ by a new family.

And this is not a joke...If the girl does not arrive with a huge dowry or is too modest and patient, then it is impossible for her to cope with the constant discontent, pressure and threats of her new relatives. The bride’s parents most often cannot or do not want to help their daughters. So, it gets to a point where they can’t stand it any longer - they go to extreme measures, seeing suicide as the only way out of their torment.

I would like to cite information from a BBC correspondent in Tajikistan, Anora Sarkorova, written back in 2012:

"Women are often pushed to take a desperate step due to beatings and abuse in their family. In Tajikistan, hundreds of women try to take their own lives every year. The main cause of suicide is family conflicts and domestic violence.

Women who decide to commit suicide are not stopped by fear of death, religious prohibitions, or fears for the future of their own children. Their methods vary: hanging, drowning and committing acts of self-immolation.

Many women saved from their suicide attempts admit that they only wanted to try and scare the household and change the attitude of the husband and his family. Yet the rate of female suicides in a country where in some regions tradition is above the law is causing concern among authorities.

According to a study conducted by Tajik human rights defenders and women's movement activists, more than half of Tajik women regularly experience domestic violence. Moreover, the statistics have remained unchanged for many years, despite the authorities' attempts to solve the problem of domestic violence..."

Every year such cases become more frequent not only in Tajikistan, but throughout Central Asia.

Let my new story give you food for thought, my dear readers.

***Yours truly,***

***Gulsifat Shakhidi***

## CHAPTER ONE:

# The böök öf Life

*I, Ozar Qurboni, wrote this book based on the diaries I kept from my school years.*

*My teachers, friends and classmates were always surprised by my memory, which captured various events. I also knew how to amaze everyone with my school essays on literature and picturesque stories in which, with interesting and meticulous detail, I would write about what was happening in our native region of Zarnisor. I confess that since early childhood, I had always dreamed of becoming a writer, and the diaries preserved my impressions, experiences and years of growing up. Now I will give this book of life to my bride, Gulbahor, to read before our wedding. I hope that my beloved will understand why I did not want to build our family life in this town - in full view of my relatives and neighbours.*

In this book, I tried to share a little about the fears instilled in me as a child. My Gulbahor, will you believe this? Doubts tormented me throughout the years of our friendship, which gradually grew into love. None of my family knew about this, I didn't even dare to tell my mother at first about my intention to marry you. As we like to say, "mice crawl through the corners of the house, and there are a pair of ears on each mouse."

We lived in the regional centre - near the Uzbek border, in a town on the outskirts of where the Tajik Aluminium Plant was built. My father, Nariman Abdullayevich Qurboni, was in charge as the chairman of the district council. Everyone respected him, and this mattered to me. But for some reason, as a teenager, I heard people laughing behind my back: they didn't call me Ozar Narimanovich, but instead, 'Ozar Akhrimanovich'. I thought, "What kind of joke is that?" And I became convinced that the nickname Akhriman had been secretly stuck to my father. I decided to look up the meaning of names in reference books and other sources. And this is what I found out:

"Nariman is translated from Arabic as 'fire-like', 'fearless', 'brave', 'strong in spirit', 'fiery warrior'. But not all fires burn bright. A man with this name is said to be endowed with great sexuality and attractiveness. He is prone to promiscuous sexual relationships and may be attracted to several partners at the same time. If his interest in a woman begins to fade, then, without hesitation, he begins to look for a replacement for her. But on the side. Nariman marries once and never again. In the family he is despotic and insists on discipline. He prefers to control everything down to the smallest detail. For his children, he is a stern but fair father. In psychology, Nariman is characterized as a person with a very changeable character and is sometimes able to do more for others than for his family."

Once, I asked my brothers why they called our father Akhriman behind his back, and me Akhrimanovich, and they looked at each other and replied: "Don't worry about that!" But I was offended and unpleased to hear my middle name in a distorted form. And once again, I turned to books. Fortunately, there was a huge library in the house.

My mother, Anvarova Sadbarg Umarovna, was a teacher of Tajik language and literature. Early in my childhood, she often talked about the ancient Persian book 'Avesta' - the sacred book of Zoroastrianism. Later, from what I read, I learned that in the early Iranian religious and Zoroastrianist texts, 'Akhriman' is known as an evil spirit, the lord of darkness and chaos, the source of human confusion, disappointment and discord. He existed in opposition to the good or bright spirit known as Ahura Mazda (Ormuzd, Hurmuz). In other, later religions, Akhriman goes by other names: Satan in Judaism, the devil in Christianity, Iblis and Shaitan in Islam.

I had a whole life ahead of me to understand the intricacies of my family's destinies. And the discoveries that I made hurt the souls of my entire family and friends.

I grew up in what seemed to be a very prosperous family. My mother is the kindest person, she was patient, taciturn and God-fearing. She didn't tell anyone anything about her experiences, and only asked us, her children, to respect our father. She said: "When you become adults you will understand more."

Sparing neither effort nor health, my mother strove to raise us to be honest, kind and intelligent. She made sure that we spent every minute of our lives doing useful things. And she considered that her main task was to give us a good education.

Mother had the four of us - three sons and a daughter. Tajiks like to name their children in rhyme - so all of us children are in tune - Khovar, Anvar, Ozar and our little sister Nilufar.

Mother told me that when I was born, dad came to the maternity hospital and shouted: "I only have sons!" But then Nilufar was born after me, and my mother always reminded my father of his words with a smile. My sister grew up to be such a wonderful girl that we all doted on her. I was also loved in my family for my fairness and peaceful nature. And I loved my mother so much that I felt her every breath. As a child, I was stupid and said that I would marry her. I would fall asleep next to her, listening to fairy tales and interesting stories from life. Mother constantly read books and infected me with her sweet 'disease.'

And most importantly, she taught us to respect our father. She said that in the East, the father is the head of the family. I once asked her, "Why is he mean to you?" She answered:

"You know, you are still a child, when you grow up you will understand. It is up to adults to sort out their relationships, and children should respect their mum and dad equally. Without dad you would not have been born."

My older brothers, Khovar and Anvar, successfully graduated from school and went to study at Dushanbe universities. They often asked mother to visit them, and when she went, she took our sister Nilufar with her. Dad had previously not allowed mother to leave the house, but now he allowed her to visit her sons. I really missed them, and during the days when my mother and sister left, time would drag on forever. It was as if there wasn't enough heat in the house; I would count the minutes until they came back. When mother finally got home, she hugged me in the doorway and promised she would also visit and care for her little Ozar when he also becomes a student. And one day before going to bed, she gently stroked my head and anxiously whispered:

"My son! I really want you to stay in Dushanbe after college. And be sure to complete graduate school, then you can get married, and I will move in with you. I'll live with you, okay?"

I nodded in agreement and even cried with joy.

When my mother was not at home, grandmother Salima (father's mother) came and called the neighbours for ritual gatherings. For some reason, dad didn't show up in the house on those days. And if he came, it would be only in the evenings, and he'd be quite tipsy. I once asked my grandmother about this. She replied: "Let my son breathe the breeze of freedom."

For a long-time I could not understand what those words meant. But I later realized why my mother's eyes were always so sad. Not only grandmother, but father's sisters, Mairam and Sairam, also believed that their handsome son and brother should have married someone else. The neighbours conveyed these words to my mother, but she just smiled and replied that her sisters-in-law were jealous.

I realized that my aunts did not love their husbands and, out of anger, ruined the lives of others. I began to notice that my father liked to be at the centre of intrigue. But mother was very restrained and did not allow herself to get into arguments. She probably knew that dad would never stand up for her.

There is a saying in the Tajik language: "Khudam shohu tab am vazir", translated as; "I am the Shah, and my desires, viziers." This is exactly what was said about our dad Nariman. I noticed that my father always did what he wanted. His word was law!

Although he looked like my father, my elder brother, Khovar, was completely different in character – he was very sympathetic and wise beyond his years. We all loved him for his kind heart. He was the protector of the family. I helped mother raise my sister and me, since our nanajon (is what we called our mother) had to work often, both at home and at school.

My brothers helped me grow up quickly, teaching me with the way they did things and their attitude to school and home. When they went off to university, they said that I would have to do everything myself from now on.

There was an eight-year gap between Anvar and me. Khovar and Anvar were the same age, and Nilufar and I were too. So, when my brothers left to study in the capital, I was left as the eldest son at just ten years old. And I realized then, just how much my brothers had protected me from many problems.

As a teenager, I already appreciated just how much strength and health my mother gave so that our family could be united and her children happy. She was a strong woman. I sensed how tough it was for her, but she never let me think badly about my father.

One day my mother was getting ready to go to Dushanbe with Nilufar to see my brothers. She asked me to look after the household and not get too bored. I saw sadness in her eyes and asked why she was so tired and didn't get enough sleep. She replied that she hadn't been able to sleep for a long time before the trip. As if she had a presentiment of how our separation would turn out...

Immediately after my mother left, grandmother Salima and my aunts, Mairam and Sairam, arrived. Grandmother loved to hold women's ritual gatherings, because her neighbours thanked her with gifts. And this time they invited many guests. I again wondered why my grandmother was doing all this without my mother.

I remember it all too well. It was a Tuesday and I was helping my grandmother and aunts. Mairam and Sairam were setting up the dastarkhwan, laying out a large tablecloth on the floor, with beautiful kurpachas - quilted narrow blankets – around it. Many neighbours were invited - young and old. My grandmother Salima was known throughout the area as Bibi-Khalifa (literally meaning 'Reading Lady'). At gatherings like these, she read and explained sacred books and told parables. When she arrived, she went straight through the living room to a small adjoining room, which was her bedroom. The aunts were in my mother's room.

Before the ceremony, grandmother usually preened herself in front of the mirror. I came in to tell her that the guests had arrived. To my surprise, she poured some vodka into a cup and, winking, said, "This is for courage," and drank it in one gulp. My jaw almost dropped. How could she do that? Drinking is prohibited by the

Koran; And she's the one that reads suras from the holy book. Then suddenly... Grandmother looked at me and laughed.

"You didn't see anything, understand?" She widened her eyes, lined with antimony, so that I was scared.

"Okay, onajon," I said, lowering my eyes.

"Well, take me to the guests," said grandmother Salima, taking me by the shoulder.

Our neighbours gathered in the living room. A place covered in many pillows was prepared for my grandmother as a place of honour, and my two aunts sat nearby. And although there was plenty of space there, the neighbours sat on the side and across from grandmother instead.

Among the guests was our closest and beloved neighbour, Aunt Parvin, who had worked as a teacher her whole life. She started as a simple nanny and later became a manager. Everyone loved her and tried to place their children in her kindergarten. Aunt Parvin's husband, Uncle Farrukh Orifov, was my father's driver and friend. About 10 years ago, dad separated a plot of land from our huge garden so that the Orifov family could build a house there. Our courtyards were connected by a common internal gate, and their son Ravshan and I grew up together, we became friends, birds of a feather. Everyone said that we even looked alike.

On the day of the gathering, Aunt Parvin brought Ravshan to help me. Later, I learned how the rite or ritual of 'Bibi Seshanbe' (literally meaning 'Lady Tuesday') was preserved in the Islamic religion.

Its roots are of pre-Islamic origin, coming from the cult of the ancient Zoroastrian goddess Anahita. During the ritual, the main reading lady tells the legend about Bibi Seshanbe, a holy woman who helped an orphan. The legend is similar to that of the fairy tale 'Cinderella' – how a poor girl wins the favour of the prince with her intelligence, beauty and kindness. For the entire time, the reader turns to the suras of the Koran, talking about holy women in Islam. In the centre of the dastarkhwan, candles burned dimly – traditionally, there needs to be 41 of them, one for each of the spirits of holy people in heaven who help women. There is usually a lot of white on the dastarkhwan: dishes made from flour and milk, sugar, salt. And the heads of all the women participating in the ritual should be covered with white scarves, symbolizing purity and a bright beginning.

The main symbol of the Bibi Seshanbe ritual is considered to be the sufra - a special mat made of leather or thick oilcloth tablecloth, on which flour is sifted when preparing the dough. It is spread on the floor three times, while standing with your back to the guests. First, the sufra is spread out with wishes for success in business, good luck and happiness. Then with a request for protection and help in opening paths in life from Mother Bibi Seshanbe. Lastly, it must be done by the mistress of the house, who must ask for help in achieving goals and solving problems.

After the ceremony, ritual dishes are served. At the end, the sufra is removed and placed on the head of the mistress of the house. When the housewife with the sufra on her head goes to the exit, she is asked: "Where are you going?" To which she replies: "To celebrate!"

It seemed to me that this ritual was only so active because it gave women the chance for spiritual comfort, and a reassuring discussion of everyday problems and their solutions. However, on that specific 'Holy Tuesday' in our home, it all turned out the complete opposite way…

My friend Ravshan and I had to constantly walk back and forth - from the kitchen to the living room and back. Our neighbour, Aunt Anora-kayvonu (or 'kadbonu', the word means hostess or manager of the dastarkhwan) ran the kitchen. On our street she was the lynchpin of home celebrations and rituals. And when Aunt Anora instructed, we took soup to the guests in large cups on trays, then pilaf on plates. They would constantly brew tea and change teapots.

Our dastarkhwan was rich with all kinds of sweets and fruits, flat-breads of various types, sambusa, homemade halva and many ritual dishes. Dad and Uncle Farrukh had really done well - buying a carload of groceries in the morning, after which he left and did not reappear until late into the night.

Ravshan and I had worked hard and at the end of the ritual we decided to sit next to Aunt Parvin. When the sufra was collected, my eldest aunt Mairam put it on her head and began to walk in front of the guests. Grandmother Salima then asked her loudly: "Where are you going, daughter?" All the guests chimed in with the same question. Smiling broadly, my aunt answered: "To celebrate, my dears!"

Then I noticed Aunt Parvin's face flush. Without looking at the aunt wearing the sufra on her head, she calmly turned to grandmother and said:

"Shouldn't Sadbarg, the mistress of the house, walk with the sufra? Why do you always have these gatherings when she's away? Your daughter Mairam should only organize these rituals in her own home – then nobody would question it."

Silence had descended in the living room. Grandmother Salima suddenly straightened up and after a short pause, answered:

"You also have the right to act as mistress if you want! Half of Nariman's plot of land was seized and a house built at his expense. And do you remember what services were offered? Maybe I should remind you?"

"There is no other mistress in this house besides Sadbarg," Aunt Parvin answered in surprise.

"Mother, please explain," said Aunt Mairam and laughed loudly. "It's no coincidence that Ozar and Ravshan look so similar after all."

"I always tell the truth to everyone's face, even if sometimes it's too hard to bear," the grandmother began.

"You know what! Truth must be reflected, first and foremost, in a person's eyes and soul, otherwise, as popular wisdom says, it might just come back around and smack you right in the face," answered Aunt Parvin. She whispered to Ravshan and me to leave the room and go into the garden.

We don't know what happened in the living room afterwards. But you could hear Aunt Parvin explaining everything very sternly and harshly while the guests stayed silent. When she finally came out, Ravshan ran after her. And from the yard nearby, I heard one neighbour say to another: “What a gathering... Though I do feel bad for poor Parvin, she also suffered thanks to her Akhriman.”

My grandmother and aunts quickly got ready to leave. An hour later, the house was silent, as if there was never a ritual gathering in the first place. I was left alone and confused. Our neighbour, aunt Anora, the hostess and manager, cleaned up and put things in order in the house. She came up to me, stroked my head and then went to Aunt Parvin.

It was already dusk, and I was still sitting on the trestle bed in the yard. Oh, how I wished then that my mother was there with me. I decided to go to Aunt Parvin. Our neighbours’ door was open. Inside, it was completely silent. I was surprised as I walked through the empty rooms. Lights were on everywhere. I went through to the backyard and suddenly heard Ravshan’s loud sobs:

“Mother, mother! Why did you do this?”

I went across the yard and looked in to the barn. Then I saw a truly terrible sight - the lifeless body of Aunt Parvin hanging right before my eyes.

I was speechless with horror - I couldn’t say a word to Ravshan. He was collapsed on his knees and it seemed that his sobs made even the sky shake with thunder. Ravshan suddenly fell over, and lost consciousness. I wanted to pick him up, but I didn’t have enough strength. I ran to get some water and poured a whole ladle on Ravshan’s head. My friend began to come to his senses. When he opened his eyes, his steely and cold gaze scared me. I helped him to his feet and led him out onto the veranda. There was a moment of long, uncomfortable silence before Ravshan quietly turned and put a letter in my pocket: "Please give this to auntie Sadbarg," was written on it.

We didn't even notice the neighbours gathering in the yard. The men took the deceased woman from the rope, carried her inside and lowered her on a bed. The women bustled around preparing the deceased for the rite of ablution and saying prayers. Domullo, the local rector of the mosque, also arrived. Only much later did the police turn up.

After sitting together in silence for a while, Ravshan eventually asked me to go home. I wanted to hug him, but he stopped me with a hard look, turned away and went into his mother's room.

I walked through the common gate into our garden and sat on the swing. My mother and Aunt Parvin often spent hot summer evenings in intimate conversations here. My head felt heavy, and as it drooped down, I noticed a letter under my feet, I must have dropped it as I sat down. I wanted to read it, but it was too dark. There were heavy clouds overhead, and the moon, as if weak with grief, could not penetrate. When thunder began to rumble, I became frightened. Trembling, I ran into the house and threw myself on the sofa. I lay in a daze for a long time, in complete silence, listening only to the loud drops of rain hitting the glass.

Eventually the gate creaked and my father, groaning, staggered onto the veranda. I heard him take off his wet clothes, change them, then run over to the neighbours. I was overcome by sleep and felt as if I was slowly falling into a deep, deep hole.

Next morning I woke up early and decided to read Aunt Parvin's letter before my mother arrived. The terrible truth about my father stabbed me in the heart. That day I got much older and even a few of my hairs turned grey, despite my youth. I decided not to show the letter to anyone and keep the secret to myself.

My mother arrived before dawn and, when she saw me, burst into tears.

"Why are you so in such a state, my son? What's happened? Did you see aunty Parvin yesterday? Did you see everything?" She asked anxiously.

I didn't answer, I just lowered my head sadly. Mother hugged me close and said quietly:

"I had a dream last night. It was as if I had climbed a mountain and found a Catholic church there. I went in and saw a statue of the Blessed Virgin Mary with a baby in her arms. I came closer, and instead of a stone baby, it was you, Ozar, reaching out to me and asking to be held in my arms. I woke up and realized that my son was feeling very bad and that he was calling me. So, I came to you, my dear. And to come back to such grief..."

Mother wiped away her tears and added tenderly:

"My poor boy..."

I hid my head on her chest and silently swallowed my tears.

From that day on I began to keep a diary. I decided to pour out my experiences only on paper, so as not to accumulate negativity in my soul.

## CHAPTER TWO:

# Aunt Parvin

I loved our neighbour, Aunt Parvin, more than any of our neighbours. And she accepted me as a son, considering our friendship with Ravshan to be brotherly.

As I already said, she worked her whole life in the best kindergarten-nursery, Gunchaho – looking after small children. She started as a nanny, then, after graduating remotely from a pedagogical institute, became a teacher, and for the last 10 years she has been Gunchaho's manager.

Many children in our town went there, and Parvin Mukhtarovna Orifova was respected by the young and the old, and the queue for places in the kindergarten was several years ahead. The institution had a great owner – a person from the aluminium plant. In the summer, the children were taken to a dacha, next to the river.

Parvin Mukhtarovna knew how to get along with both children and adults. No one had ever heard a harsh word from her. Restrained and tactful, with a soft and quiet voice, she attracted others to her. Aunt Parvin was not considered a beauty, but she was very pretty and always well-groomed. Even at home, she walked around with beautifully styled hair, tinted eyebrows and kohl-lined eyes. She did not dress flashily, but everything suited her and she suited it. Moreover, her gait was light and her back straight, as if she did gymnastics as a child.

Uncle Farrukh loved his family very much. Everyone always said that he was a good owner, and that his house was warm and hearty.

Ravshan's older sisters, Madina and Amina, were already married and lived in Uzbekistan. Once upon a time there were no borders: Tajiks and Uzbeks lived side by side, freely and calmly visiting one another, seeing how their relatives were doing. Then, with the acquisition of sovereignty by the Asian republics, checkpoints and customs offices with border guards sprung up everywhere.

I remember having lots of fun and dancing at his sisters' weddings, and that I was jealous of my friend, because he already had nephews – even though we were the same age, he was already an uncle. We babysat and played with the kids together. Now Madina and Amina and their children rarely came, and Ravshan was worried that due to the closure of the borders, he had less contact with his family.

Aunty Parvin was my mother's best friend. I've heard many times how, during their intimate conversations, she thanked my mother for her help and encouragement to finish college and receive a higher pedagogical education.

We had a huge garden. When dad began to move up the career ladder and was given a company car, he brought his classmate Farrukh Orifov to work with him; Uncle Farrukh was from a simple large family and was unable to continue his university studies.

He had trained as a professional driver and earned money from a young age, supporting his parents. Seeing his difficult situation and the cramped conditions in his parents' house, dad invited Farrukh to build his own home on our land. Uncle Farrukh's entire family was grateful. He and others who respected my father called him Rais (meaning - boss, chief). It was quite convenient for my father - the car was always ready and the driver was nearby.

After some time, Mother and Aunt Parvin became very good friends, and Ravshan and I became inseparable. Any time there were events in the city, we always went together. Aunt Parvin was with my mother in both sorrow and joy and did not allow anyone to humiliate or offend her.

One time, at a school parents meeting, where children were also present, an unpleasant incident occurred. Aunt Parvin was sitting with Ravshan, and my mother, as a teacher, was sat next to me.

Our home-room teacher spoke at the meeting about the students, noting both the good and the shortcomings. Suddenly, the mother of one of the students jumped up and began screaming about the unfair treatment of her daughter. My mother, an eternal peacemaker, tried to gently explain that it was not right to bring these things up with the teacher in front of the children. But the woman waved her hand contemptuously and rudely interrupted:

"You haven't a clue what I'm talking about! Stay out of my business. I can deal with my own problems."

Mother sank a little, and Aunt Parvin clasped her friend's hand and, getting up swiftly, asked all the children to leave the class with a sweet smile. The conversation continued behind closed doors. Our classmates Saodatka and Lenka tried to eavesdrop and then told us that Parvin Mukhtarovna seemed to have reconciled the parents and teachers. After the meeting, my excited mother hugged her friend and whispered:

"My dear neighbour, thank you for your support! It's as if you read my thoughts, you know and understand everything."

Aunt Parvin lowered her sad eyes and quietly answered:

"We have been close for so many years and our souls have grown together, like family. Of course, I know that you, Sadbarg, deserve to be treated well. If you take other people's negative words to heart, you'd be carrying mountains of sorrow on your shoulders. Shall we go home and have some tea?"

I also remembered the incident with my brother Anvar, a keen footballer. During training, his shoes got really worn out and there wasn't enough time to change into sneakers, so he instead played barefoot. But one time, he got carried away and injured the big toe of his right foot. The nail came off and was barely hanging on by a thread. Fortunately, Parvin was nearby: without wasting a second, she picked the tall Anvar up in her arms and carried him to an emergency room. There, his nail was removed and his toe bandaged.

When mother eventually saw them on the doorstep, she alarmed:

"What happened, son? Why are there bandages on your foot?"

"Anvar was in such a hurry to get home that he slipped and injured his nail. Don't worry dear, the boy is doing well now," our beloved

Aunt answered, smiling at Anvar.

It always seemed to me that Aunt Parvin was very protective of my mother. Honestly, I couldn't understand why? In our town, everyone respected and appreciated their beloved teacher Sadbarg Umarovna, because many were her students and parents of students.

But it turned out that mother also had ill-wishers, or rather, ill-wishing women. They believed that since my mother humbly tolerated the whims and betrayals of her husband, it meant that she allowed others to treat her with disdain.

But if one person or another tried to insult my mother in public, Aunt Parvin would immediately come to her friend's defence. In my memory, pictures were formed from individual- coloured pieces of glass like in a kaleidoscope. Here is one:

The town held a fair and sale of folk crafts once a month. Mother and Aunt Parvin were constantly shopping to fill their children's wedding chests with beautiful things. This is one of our Eastern customs - collecting a 'dowry' for boys and girls almost from when they're still in a cradle.

Sometimes Ravshan and I were taken to the fair. Our mothers lingered especially at the stalls with skullcaps and colourful robes. Mother was always looking for 'chusti' skullcaps (from the city, Chust) of an ancient type: low, dark grey, with discreet ornamental embroidery of cucumbers or almonds. But for some reason, folk craftswomen sewed very high skullcaps: it seems that they were for short men, so that they would appear taller.

We were already well known on this row of stalls. One day, I witnessed quite a scene. Mother had just asked the sellers if the craftswomen had finished her order, when suddenly we heard a mocking remark loudly and deliberately shouted behind us:

"Oh, it's so difficult with such capricious men!"

Mother and Aunt Parvin turned towards the voice. Standing at the stall opposite was Halima Akhmadovna, the chief accountant of the aluminium plant. At that time, as a teenager, I did not understand why she was not respected in our town. She was pretty, well-groomed and rich. She was the first of the townspeople to buy a new Volga and she drove it herself. We boys watched with envy as she sat behind the wheel driving such a large car in style. It was even awkward to call her aunt, so we only referred to her by her first name and patronymic.

The saleswoman glanced briefly at Halima Akhmadovna, who was sorting through the skullcaps, and answered:

"Many people here ask for that exact skullcap model, but alas, almost no one sews them these days."

Halima Akhmadovna proudly raised her eyebrows and said with a grin, as it seemed to me, in our direction:

"I have everything! And what I don't have, I can and will always get. I choose a gift for the purpose of pleasing my man. That model is exactly the kind of skullcap that he likes! It looks like I'll have to learn how to embroider and craft so that I can make it myself."

"It'd be better if you gave him a child as a gift, and so you won't be left alone," the saleswoman advised with a chuckle.

"I would give birth, but he refuses to bare the fruits of our love. Every time I bring it up he threatens to leave me, but I don't want to lose him. You know how handsome he is, right? Alain Delon would cry with envy if he saw him!"

"So marry him then!" The saleswoman again gave her advice.

"What are you saying?! He is afraid of ruining his career. And he's no husband! He has already tormented his current wife; And one woman is never enough for him, I'm not the only one who knows that."

I noticed how my mother shuddered at these words. And Aunt Parvin immediately hugged the three of us by the shoulders and asked us to go to the food aisle. She turned to that stall with the skullcaps, where Halima Akhmadovna stood with a triumphant look. I don't know what they started talking about, but I learned about the fate of that woman only ten years later.

I was already studying at the philological department of the Tajik State University, and in my third year, during the holidays, I did an internship at the aluminium plant. According to the law on the state language, documents must be prepared and maintained in Tajik language. So philologists became necessary at the aluminium plant.

That day I learned that the chief accountant, Halima Akhmadovna, died after giving birth from bleeding. Everyone got ready to go to the wake, and so did I.

Halima Akhmadovna's old mother sobbed bitterly:

"God almighty, why do you put me through such trials? It was my turn to die. Oh, Lord, why don't you punish Akhriman? Why should he, the embodiment of evil, live and kill everyone around him? What will happen to my newborn granddaughter?" Raising her hands to the sky, she wailed.

It seemed to me that everyone was looking in my direction. I turned and left.

After reading Aunt Parvin's letter, I understood a lot. And now I think I can tell you how it all happened.

The kindergarten where Aunt Parvin worked at was located a house away from our home. My father was a very busy man, and so my mother took us and brought us there. And when we older, we ran there and back ourselves.

But sometimes my father would pick me up with Ravshan in the car and entrusted Uncle Farrukh to take us to the river and feed us shashlik. He himself would go home on foot.

But he came home long after we returned. No one knew where he had been and where he came from. Uncle Farrukh told me that the same thing happened before with his daughters and my older brothers: a ride to the river and a shashlik treat.

Now I know why father Nariman distracted us.

My father was always surrounded by attentive women; he liked that everyone looked at him with admiration and considered him handsome. But not Aunt Parvin. She treated him as a friend and neighbour - evenly and without servility. And my father was one of those men who could not tolerate something like that. Always, and at any cost, he sought to subjugate the obstinate the women around him. His next target just happened to be our dear aunt Parvin.

Should I be judging my elders? I have no right. But I am a witness to what happened and still think it is right to tell the truth.

My father did a good deed by settling his friend's family nearby, and they all doted on him. In gratitude, our beloved aunt often treated us to the most delicious and delectable dishes. Mother would often say:

"Dear neighbour, you are spoiling us!"

And she would return with a dish full of apricots from our garden, which Aunt Parvin loved so much.

"I have two assistant daughters in the kitchen, so we cook with six hands," my mother's friend smiled in response. "Your youngest, Nilufar, will grow up and also spoil us." When Ravshan's sisters got married and left, Mother and Aunt Parvin began to use the services of our neighbour Anora-kayvonu.

These days I have come to these conclusions: it turns out that my father specifically helped Uncle Farrukh so he could get Parvin's body, to amaze her with his generosity and nobility. In response, though, there was only sincere gratitude, nothing more.

Once my father went to the wedding of his subordinate and took Uncle Farrukh with him, who always refused to drink alcohol. But that fateful evening he drank, and the owners of the house left the weakened guest to lie on the veranda and come to his senses.

Let me quote from memory an excerpt from Aunt Parvin's letter:

*"It was the most terrible day of my life. I know how painful it will be for you to read this, my dear neighbour, but you must know the truth. Nariman came from the wedding to our home, alone without his friend, without my Farrukh. I was in a hurry. When I decided to look for my drunken husband, he stopped me, squeezing my hands painfully. It's hard to even retell what happened later. That day was the day I learned what violence is. This went on for a long time, and I prayed to God to take me to him.*

*After it was all over, Rais threw himself on his knees and apologized. He swore that Satan had suddenly possessed him. And it will never happen again. He promised that not a single living soul would know about this. That all his life he will remember what sin he committed. I wanted to die even then, but I thought about my daughters and my beloved Farrukh. I kicked out my neighbour and, having washed off the dirt, went to fetch my husband.*

*And, it's true, Rais didn't touch me anymore, but he always looked in my direction with some kind of disdain, like a winner. I found out later that I was pregnant and wanted to have an abortion. But the doctors did not allow it. Nine months later Ravshan was born...*

*I sometimes heard Rais loudly 'joking' that, thanks to him, many families had sons. Everyone laughed, taking it as a joke. Now I know how much pain and sin he brought not only to me.*

*I loved you and your children and didn't tell you anything then. Nariman, who promised to remain silent about his sin, still did not keep his word. He told his mother about all his 'victories'. And with this terrible truth, which I hid and feared for so many years, I was publicly reproached.*

*I wrote everything in a farewell letter to Farrukh. I believe he loves me and will forgive me. And I pray to God that he and Ravshan go away from here..."*

Only God knows how much pain and shock I felt reading these lines. Many things were difficult for me as a teenager to understand. So, Ravshan is my brother? I will never forget his look that night: he must have read his mother's last letters!

On the day of the funeral, my mother was at Aunt Parvin's house, and I was worried about her. I was afraid that someone would offend her with an evil word. I thought that now there was only me left to protect my mother.

Mother sat next to Ravshan on the trestle bed and cried, not letting him go from her. He looked at the veranda, where next to the stretcher the neighbours were mourning Aunt Parvin, seeing her off on her last journey. I went up to my friend. He took my hand and I felt better.

It seemed our entire town had gathered at Uncle Farrukh's house. Ravshan's sisters - Madina and Amina – were also there. I was appalled by the wave of grief that filled this house. Father sat with the leaders of the city and the aluminium plant. All the women were in dark robes, the men, in black chapans (robes) and skullcaps.

My father, uncle Farrukh and his sons-in-law began to carry out the stretcher with the deceased. Others lined up to take over on the way to the cemetery. With tears and lamentations, the funeral procession was accompanied by the female neighbours only as far as the gate of the cemetery, because according to our laws they are not allowed to enter.

Ravshan decided to accompany my mother on her last journey, and I am with him. Mother stopped us, opened her clenched fist, and asked with tears:

"My dears, take these apricot kernels and throw them into the ground - next to Parvin's resting place."

On the way, Ravshan asked me if I had given the letter to my mother.

"No, I read it myself and decided not to give it to her," I answered guiltily.

"I haven't given mine to dad yet either," Ravshan said quietly. We reached the cemetery. Aunt Parvin was quickly buried. Ravshan managed to throw some seeds onto the grave and said:

"Mother loved your apricots very much, and Aunt Sadbarg gave me these seeds, so I hope to God, that at least one tree will grow here from them."

Indeed, all our neighbours had apricots, but in our garden, they were especially famous for their unusual taste and colour. My mother told me that the first owner of this garden, back in pre-revolutionary times, at the end of the 19th century, crossed a tree with cuttings separated from plants that were grown from seeds brought from abroad. Many then took the seeds of the fruit and planted the sprouts of our tree, crossed them, but were never able to replicate that taste. They say that the old merchant owner even brought foreign soil in a large clay jug of olive oil.

Aunt Parvin called these fruits heavenly. And now, she is most definitely in the Garden of Eden, because during her lifetime she was called 'bihishti,' that is, the earthly representative of paradise. No one, neither at the wake or later, spoke about that incident in our house and they remembered her only with kind words. Although, who knows, everyone is different after all...

...Ravshan and I were left alone in the cemetery and stood silently at the grave. Suddenly thunder struck and rain started pouring down. We had to run home under lashing streams and flashes of lightning. We were soaked to the skin. Mother was waiting for us at the gate. You could see how worried she was:

"Why did it take you so long? Children should not be left alone in the cemetery. Go and change your clothes, otherwise you'll catch a cold!

"Aunt Sadbarg, we are no longer children," Ravshan answered quietly.

"Yes, my dears, grief has already made you older" my mother cried and hugged us tightly.

After the funeral, on the fortieth day, a terrible thing happened. First, there was an explosion in my father's official car, and then Uncle Farrukh's house burned down. I rushed into their yard, but my neighbours were already getting into a minibus. Ravshan ran up to me and managed to say:

"We are leaving for Uzbekistan and going to our relatives, we will live next to our sisters. That's what dad decided."

And he added quietly:

"I gave him my mother's letter, and I beg you not to make my mistake. Don't let Aunt Sadbarg know the truth… I don't want another tragedy."

We both cried and hugged each other tightly. I didn't know that this was my last meeting with Ravshan, with his father and sisters. There were rumours that Uncle Farrukh could not obtain a citizenship in Uzbekistan for a long time, so instead, he applied to the Russian Embassy and became a Russian citizen, living somewhere in the Russian outback. Someday I will find my friend, and we will meet again.

On the day of our farewell, I recounted Aunt Parvin's letter in my diary. I was especially struck by the last lines on the very bottom of the page:

*"My dear and beloved Sadbarg, you are simply a saint! You endure all of life's trials as the Almighty commanded us. Not only do you raise your children, but you also teach your students nobility, mercy and understanding. I see this as an example of how to treat my own children.*

*Don't judge me for leaving like this. But I can no longer and do not want to live with a sin that I do not consider myself guilty of. I am a strong woman, but our society is imperfect. I ask for God, all my family and friends to forgive me for what I have done. Most of all, I ask Allah to be merciful to my kind surroundings and loved ones."*

A huge apricot tree grew on Aunt Parvin's grave. Every year it yields a plentiful crop of orange-gold, delicious fruit, which the local children feast on. Girls and boys both take care of the grave, watering the tree to make sure it never dries out. The elderly try to remind us that women and children are not allowed in the cemetery, but they understand that time makes its own adjustments.

## CHAPTER THREE:

Mother told me that her first-born, Khovar, is the fruit of her sincere love and that is why he is very similar to his father. And he was more like him than the rest of us.

Everywhere - among friends, among classmates, and on the school football team, Khovar was a leader. As his younger siblings, we loved him very much, he was our protector and educator.

When I was born, my mother could not stay on maternity leave for long, because there was no one to replace her at school. As a high school student, Khovar had to become my nanny. His friends cheerfully teased him and said that he looked like Sergei Prokhanov, the hero of the film 'Moustached Nanny.' Khovar was not offended and in response, contentedly pinched his barely visible moustache.

Mother recalled how Khovar even put her dresses on so that I could fall asleep peacefully. He often took me in a stroller through the streets, singing funny songs, and then assured my family that I winked at him with a smile.

My brother and mother would take shifts looking after me, my brother for the first half, after which he would study, and my mother for the second half, after she came home from work. Khovar also brought me to school in a stroller and passed me from one pair of hands to another. Mother constantly repeated that without such a nice and reliable assistant it would be difficult for her. And then when mother had our little sister Nilufar, she found herself in Khovar's care too.

Aunt Parvin was looking after Ravshan at the same time and so knew from experience how difficult it was for her friend Sadbarg. As soon as I turned a year old, she accepted me in her nursery. And I, right from the cradle, grew up with Ravshan.

In the mornings, Uncle Farrukh would take Aunt Parvin and me to the nursery. In the evenings, my brothers took me home, and our neighbour came back with Ravshan a little later - she was always very busy.

Looking at it now, it seems to me that Khovar has in many ways, replaced our father. Dad Nariman was never at home, he was busy with his career and considered his work to be the most important thing in his life. I was firmly convinced that since ancient times, everyday problems and raising children were the tasks and responsibilities of women.

From an early age, Khovar realized the injustice of such a division of responsibilities and strove to help his mother in everything. He was wise beyond his years and knew how to convince anyone in an argument and 'settle' an unpleasant situation. Khovar never said anything bad about anyone and taught us this. At school he was one of the best. His friends called him Khovar-nadega (meaning - reliable). Our grandmother Salima, my father's mother, said that he was the only one that looked like he was from their side of the family. The fact is that mother had huge light brown eyes, and dad had black and slanted ones. Khovar's were a beautiful mix of both. I can't count how many girls fell in love with him. But most importantly, his classmate Amina, Ravshan's sister, loved him. And it was mutual.

After tenth grade, Khovar entered university, the Faculty of Oriental Studies. After taking the entrance exams, only the top 50 students were accepted, and my brother was one of them. And as for Amina, she went to university in the city of Termez, in Uzbekistan, where her grandmother lived. That's what her parents decided. Aunt Parvin was from an old Tajik family, and all her ancestors lived in Termez from as long as anyone could remember.

Everyone seemed to rejoice in the wonderful relationship between Amina and Khovar. Surely, they would be married soon? But then came the spectacle that was 'independence', with new borders dividing Tajiks and Uzbeks into friends and foes. Traveling abroad and visiting relatives became problematic. Suddenly, Aunt Parvin began talking about how Amina would stay with her grandmother after college, and that Khovar would not move in with them. No one could understand why Amina calmly accepted such a decision.

Khovar was very upset and so was mother. But everything was made clear as I looked through that last letter from Aunt Parvin, in which she asked for forgiveness from my mother:

*"My dear Sadbarg, now you must understand why I was against Amina's wedding with Khovar. Just one of those looks from his father was enough for me to understand that Amina would not be safe. And Nariman's words: "I hope that Amina is as good as her mother," alarmed me so much I felt a sharp pain in my heart. Could I really allow my daughter to suffer the same fate as me? So, I decided to send both of my girls to Uzbekistan, to my mother. I was afraid for them.*

*You always protected your husband. People said that he only became unconsciously vile when he was drinking. But that when he was sober he was good. It's true what they say, love makes us blind. Nariman is used to acting with impunity. He thinks of himself as the top dog, for whom everything is allowed. He was raised from childhood like this. And there are many in our circle who endorse this. More than once, I have heard people say: "If Nariman were such a bad person, would he have lived so well and become so successful?" No one cares that the well-being of his family rests on the sacrifices you make. Nariman attributes all his success in life to himself alone. But God will not tolerate this for long. When he finally falls from grace, you will be blamed by everyone for all of Nariman's failures. So please, take care of yourself, my dear..."*

I constantly caught myself thinking: it's good I didn't give my mother the letter. Ravshan was right - another tragedy would have certainly happened.

...Khovar decided to talk things over with Amina. But he couldn't convince his beloved. She left for Termez with another man, now her husband, and Madina soon followed. Khovar wanted to continue his studies in graduate school. He always carried a photograph of Amina with him.

I remember my older brother in the best days of his youth, when he was the life and soul of any group or event. He was handsome, lively with neither wine nor cigarettes, generous and with a great sense of humour. My brother's erudition amazed everyone. On a dare, he could solve any crossword puzzle in just five minutes. His fascinating stories about the history of ancient civilizations! The many poems he recited by heart! And his excellent command of English, Arabic, Persian!

It seemed that my brother had no equal. Thanks to him, I found out about a great writer of the 'lost generation'. We talked about Erich Remarque for a long time before going to bed. It seems to me that he himself could become a talented writer, because his stories were always incredibly interesting. Noticing that I was getting sleepy, he repeated his favourite quote from his revered Remarque: "You can talk about happiness for five minutes, no more. There is nothing to say here except that you are happy. But people can talk about misfortune all night long." And, covering me with a blanket, he added:

"Good night, brother! Grow up quickly!"

Already in his fourth year as the best student, they wanted to send him to one of the Arab countries to work at an embassy. But it didn't work out... Either Khovar's successes haunted envious people, or the 'competent authorities' tried to test his strength – but whoever it was, they ended up putting dangerous 'additives' in his drink, though now there's no way to know for sure who it was. Before flying out, my brother and friends celebrated the beginning of his diplomatic career and at some point... Khovar passed out, losing consciousness after the first drink. He woke up in a drug treatment clinic, where our mother came for him. Khovar's future was ruined. The authorities put him on a 'blacklist'. Khovar withdrew into himself. He began to drink and wept bitterly. All his classmates went on business trips abroad, and he, who graduated with honours, could only be a simple schoolteacher. He decided to put graduate school on hold, probably knowing deep down that his dreams of continuing his studies were shattered forever.

Father blamed my mother for Khovar's drunkenness. Grandmother Salima also added fuel to the fire. But I have seen with my own eyes more than once how she went out to religious ceremonies after drinking a cup of vodka. I remember how she expressed her thought to my mother with displeasure:

"Do you not teach other children to be smart and responsible, dear daughter-in-law. What about your own children? If your firstborn became a drunkard, what would happen to the rest?"

"That's your grandson! You're talking about him as if about a stranger. We should work together to save him from this destructive urge," my mother protested silently in her heart.

But our grandmother wouldn't relent:

"I raised a very fine man, even without a higher education. Everyone knows that my Nariman is wonderful, and many dote on even the locks of his hair. And you, a teacher with such and such experience, were unable to raise a normal son."

"For me, all my children are the best! Remember how you always said that Khovar was the most like his father?" Mother was indignant.

"His face is, yes, but apart from that..." Grandmother curled her lips contemptuously and shook her head disapprovingly.

Khovar understood that his drunkenness upset everyone, especially his mother, but he could not overcome his addiction. Mother tried to treat him and took him to the hospital several times. After the IV drips, Khovar got better for several days, but the deep mental wound gave no rest, and once again, my brother reached for a glass. This continued until I entered university. I wonder how it must have felt as a mother-teacher to see her son dying from alcohol? Khovar started having problems at school and so eventually he left to go and work in Russia. He settled in Gatchina and built dachas. He met a girl there, Vera, and they got married.

Vera fell in love with him at first sight, seeing an extraordinary man with a broad soul. She worked as a mathematics teacher in college and Khovar got a job there as a teacher of history and English. The young couple lived in the house of Vera's parents, although they did not immediately support their daughter's decision to marry a Tajik. But their objections didn't last long. Gradually everything got better, and Vera's parents fell in love with Khovar as if he was their own son. We learned about this from letters that he sent us. And then Khovar and Vera came to visit us, and everyone was happy to see the young couple together. Father Nariman was the only one who couldn't even be bothered to meet them, disappearing to the capital for a meeting at the ministry, and then to grandmother's home. Mother was surprised he would not see his son. But then at the same time, she was glad in a way: without our father, there would be no scandals, and no one would offend the young people.

Our Anvar was in Dushanbe at that time, and he met his brother and Vera at the airport. He waved them off to Zarnisor, and then remained to resolve an issue at his graduate school. He promised to come home in a couple of days.

Mother became very friendly with our kind daughter-in-law and began to call her Verajon. Mother's eyes haven't sparkled with so much joy for a very long time.

"As long as Khovar doesn't lose his temper and start drinking again-" Vera quietly shared with my mother. "Then we might have a baby soon."

But Khovar heard and responded with the words of his revered Remarque: "As long as a person does not give up, he is stronger than his fate." The young couple asked mother to move to Gatchina with them, although they did not have their own housing.

"Your place is already cramped. If you ever get a separate apartment, I will certainly come and be a nanny for my first grandson. I've received my pension, so I can at least move whenever I want," my mother dreamed. "I only continue to work because there are not enough teachers, and they won't let me go while I'm at school."

"I'll come with you too," I said to support my mother.

"And what exactly is it you want? Maybe I should give you the key to the flat where I keep my money?" Khovar joked with an Ostap Bender catchphrase.

And our sister Nilufar hugged her brother and his wife and said:

"Get an apartment quickly, and we will come to visit you!"

Vera took the girl's face in her hands and said with a smile:

"Nilufar, you are so beautiful! Khovar wouldn't stop talking about you, and here I thought, of course he would praise his beloved sister, what brother doesn't? But it turns out you are a hundred times more beautiful than in the photos. Do you want to be friends?"

"Of course, dear yangajon (is what they call the elder brother's wife)," answered Nilufar, embarrassed.

When we got together, my mother was overcome with happiness. For two days, our neighbour and hostess at home celebrations, Anora-kayvonu, helped my mother in the kitchen prepare the most delicious dishes. And Vera, like a true eastern daughter-in-law, did not just stand aside. Together with Nilufar, she brought cleanliness and order to the house and yard.

"Khovar, how lucky you are with your wife. Be happy! I pray for the both of you. I wish your father was here to see you now!" Mother couldn't be happier.

On the last day before the young couple left, dad arrived with grandmother Salima.

Seeing our happy faces at the table set in the middle of the courtyard, they were either surprised or dumbfounded. Apparently, they didn't expect such a heartwarming family picture. Vera-yangajon was serving cups of tea in Tajik attire, while Anora-kayvonu carried a huge dish of pilaf. Everyone stood up respectfully, greeting their father and grandmother. Our mother, under the gaze of grandmother, seemed to hunch up and smile forcefully:

"Good evening! It's so good that you came. Tomorrow Khovar and Verajon are leaving." And as if to herself she added, "It's unfortunate I had such a terrible dream today..."

"What is this about a dream? What about?" Grandmother Salima leered, without bothering to answer the greeting.

"There is no point in telling everyone about your dreams, it's as insignificant as running water," my mother answered calmly. "Come on in, onajon. You're just in time for the pilaf."

"Well, hello my children!" The father greeted everyone grandly but did not even look in Vera's direction, treating her as if she was not there. "It's been a long time since we all got together. Grandmother and I are full. We've just eaten. We'll go outside for tea."

And then they went out to the veranda. There was silence. Mother tried to smooth out the awkwardness by inviting everyone to some pilaf and was the first to start eating. Everyone followed her example, and again the table became joyful and at ease.

Anora-kayvonu carried a large tray of fruit to the veranda, then came back in and joined us for dinner. She did this extremely rarely. She sat at the table only with those whom she considered her loved ones.

We couldn't stop looking at Khovar and Vera: it was clear how good they were together. My brother became the same cheerful person he used to be, telling stories and jokes, and we laughed out loud.

I felt that something was bothering my mother and asked her about the dream. She waved it off: our people say that women's dreams should not be believed.

"It shouldn't be a problem if you tell us, right?" Khovar inquired.

"Alright then, in my dream I saw a woman appear in my bedroom and wake me up, pointing to the floor. When I looked down, I saw a snake slithering out from under the bed. Frightened, I get off the bed and try to grab the viper by the tail. But it bites my hand. I suck and spit out the poison. That is how I save myself. I then catch the snake and hit it against the wall so mercilessly that its head turns to mush. This made me feel bad and I woke up..."

"Oh, that's horrible! What a terrifying dream," Anora-kayvon shook her head. "It looks like you have an enemy that you will defeat."

Seeing Salima grandmother come inside and approach the table, Anora-apa hastily stood up, took a dish and went to the kitchen. We also stood up, expressing respect.

"So, daughter-in-law, you dreamt of a snake? Did you get rid of it and win? A person sometimes frees themselves from all misfortunes at the cost of their life," Grandmother said, sneering. Mother hadn't time to reply before Khovar turned to his grandmother with a smile and said:

"Onajon, we haven't seen each other for so many years, I think we have other things we could be talking about. And it's better not to be afraid of death; God gives and God takes away – that's what you always said. Today let's talk about life. Here, meet Vera, my wife."

Vera smiled too. But in response, grandmother Salima launched into a tirade. Vera did not know the Tajik language, but she understood everything even without translation. Each sentence began with the word 'urus' - meaning 'Russian'.

Mother couldn't stand it and objected:

"I'm Tajik, but do you really love me? All my life people have said that it would be better if your son married a Russian rather than me. It's not a matter of nationality, is it? Now that your grandson chose the better nationality, shouldn't you be happy?"

"What's going on?" Father said angrily when he appeared in the yard. "How dare you behave like this? Where is the respect for elders in the family? Is this the attitude you teach your children?"

"No matter what happened, mother always taught us to treat you with care and respect," I unexpectedly objected to my father.

But he didn't even glance in my direction and continued in a bitter rapture:

"Who have I been working for all my life? The house, the garden - everything you have is from me! I am fulfilling my main duty. And you live with everything prepared for you and you don't even appreciate it!"

"Did mother sit at home doing nothing? She worked too," Khovar answered, trying to reassure his father. "Every man creates a family and everyone is obliged to take care of its provision. We support our families, our children will support their families. But what is a family without a woman? Do you know what my favourite writer, Remarque, said about this? "A woman is not metal furniture; she is a flower. She doesn't want to be business-like. She needs sunny, sweet words. It's better to say something nice to her every day than to work all your life with gloomy frenzy."

"You ungrateful-! Now you're here trying to teach me something?!"

Father frantically ran up to mother:

"Was it you, Sadbarg, that taught our children this insolence towards their father?" He swung his hand at her angrily, but Anvar intercepted, and Khovar and I immediately shielded my mother.

"Father, you stood up for your mother. We stand up for ours. Calm down!" Anvar said firmly.

"My mother is your grandmother! Don't you dare compare them! And I'll deal with my wife myself!"

"Your wife? No one is arguing against that. But she is also our mother. And respect begins with the mother - these were your own words," Anvar calmly answered.

Father had raised his hand to mother for the first time. And I was frightened. He had previously always held back, showing his good upbringing, intelligence, and decency. But now, his true essence of tyranny had revealed itself. Nilufar was terrified by this outburst of anger. Our little sister turned white as chalk. Tears rolled from her open eyes. Nilufar's trust in her father was rocked from that moment on.

Vera stood silently, biting her lips. Khovar hugged her and turned to his father:

"Remember how grandmother swore that you had a good-for-nothing son who was just a drunk? You and her blamed mother for everything and considered me a complete loser. It was Vera who helped me and pulled me out of my destructive passion. Now I am a respected teacher in Gatchina. Doesn't this matter to you? Just be patient - we're leaving tomorrow. Why make a scandal? So that only negativity remains in your memory?"

My brother took Vera by the hand and led her into the house. Mother followed. Nilufar cried quietly. And through clenched teeth, father said that he would take grandmother home and stay with her.

The next morning, Khovar and Vera left for Dushanbe. Mother and Anvar went with them to the plane. Nilufar and I were left alone. She secretly wiped away her tears. It seemed to me that my beloved sister had suddenly grown older. We discussed what had happened for a long time, and I realized that Nilufar was already thinking about her destiny as a woman.

# CHAPTER FOUR:

Of the three of us, the wisest, most taciturn, reasonable, sincere and generous is Anvar, our middle brother. His friends always said he had a heart the size of a watermelon, but I thought it was the size of the universe. Since childhood, people had come to him with their problems and various questions and received accurate and useful advice.

Anvar was the best chess player, and he was nicknamed Maradona for his love of football. He was an excellent student, and his mother proudly hid his report-book at the end of each school year to pass on to her future grandchildren. Anvar joked that she would have to wait a long time for grandchildren: he had no time to think about children, because there were so many things ahead. I didn't really understand nor notice the attention of the girls who wrote love notes to him. Anvar had no time for them; his head was only occupied with mathematics.

Anvar kept all our household appliances working and fixed any malfunctions himself. He even helped his neighbours repair washing machines, refrigerators, and televisions and earned himself the title 'jack of all trades.'

My brother taught me a lot too. When I grew up, he helped me figure out computer programming. We even created our own websites together. He then received an order for an official website from the management of the aluminium smelter and completed the job brilliantly.

Anvar himself was like a walking computer. He may not have read as many books as Khovar, but he knew so much. My brothers complemented each other. Khovar was tall, thin, hot-tempered, and Anwar was shorter, but strongly built, calm and taciturn. It seemed to me that he could see right through a person and understand them at once. Anvar is the only one of us who father actually listened to. Mother was right when she said:

"Our children are our strictest judges."

Anvar developed an early talent for entrepreneurship. As a tenth-grader, he opened a repair shop for household and electronic appliances. The townspeople were very grateful, because previously they had to transport equipment to Dushanbe or simply throw it away.

My brother organized the work professionally: he obtained a legal license, completed the paperwork, found good suppliers and ordered all the spare parts for repairs in advance. He even got partners. Anvar was the first of us to earn good money and provided many of the local young men with work. Our mathematician calculated everything correctly!

My brother spoke little, but to the point, and coined his own sayings. Once, after a football match, he came home with his kit ripped and filthy. Mother lamented:

“Son, why are you so messy?”

And he answered cheerfully:

“No smoke without fire, no Anvar without dirt!”

In the summer, because of the heat, all the boys in the town had their hair cut, but Anvar really did not like this. His head was so round that his friends made fun of him with the nickname, ‘globe-head,’ though my brother was not offended. Once, he picked peaches of the ‘Arapchik’ variety in our garden, popularly called ‘bald ones’, and treated them to his friends.

“Do they taste good?” He asked the boys.

“Very good!” They answered in unison.

“And wouldn’t you say we look alike: bald peach and bald Anvar,” my brother said cheerfully.

Everyone laughed together. After that, no one teased Anvar with the whole ‘globe’ thing. Mother wrote down all his funny ‘quotes’ in a notebook.

After finishing school, my brother went to Dushanbe to study at the university. He was a gold medallist, aced his interview and was accepted into the Faculty of Physics and Mathematics without having to do exams. He was given a bigger scholarship, and by his third year was already teaching freshmen. At first, he was dubbed 'muallim' – meaning teacher, as a joke, but it later it turned into a sign of great respect.

He never showed off his feelings and experiences. And he knew how to console others with the wise Solomon phrase "Everything passes. This too shall pass." Mother's anxiety would immediately leave when she heard Anvar's simple and precise words. He was sensitive and perceptive, and his mathematical thinking even helped him in relationships with family and friends.

The scandal caused by grandmother Salima before the departure of Khovar and Vera was etched in my memory. And especially the sharp image of my father's hand, swinging towards my mother's face. Anvar had blocked the blow and Father Nariman had suppressed his rage, but he did not stay at home. He left with our grandmother for Dushanbe.

After that dinner, mother couldn't stop weeping. Anvar hugged her and quietly asked:

"Why did you try to put up with this for so many years? Maybe you should have left father at the start?"

Mother shook her head sadly:

"I was young and didn't understand many things. I really did love your father. Without him I wouldn't have had such beautiful children. You are all my greatest wealth."

"There are no equations that cannot be solved," Anvar calmly objected. "Exact sciences teach us to think precisely. If you don't, you might just go crazy. If you value us, then live for us.

Don't torment yourself. We certainly can't replace father, but even without him, we are strong when it comes to solving our family equation. Believe me, mother, your peace of mind is in our hands today. But you must understand, father Nariman will never change. That's just how it is. If he was really sorry for what he had done, he'd have apologised or left a long time ago. You must accept it; it's too late to change him. We are with you, and that is the most important fact!"

And mother calmed down.

Somehow the explanation was so concise and natural that it was impossible not to listen to Anvar. He spoke clearly, as if he was solving a problem. And he helped me recover after that family scandal. Feeling my confusion and depression, my brother shook me by the shoulders and looked into my eyes in a special way:

"Do you think that worrying about a situation will improve it? If we can't correct something that is not within our power, then we might as well use what happened as life experience. And avoid making the same mistakes in the future. Do you agree?"

I nodded and wiped my tears.

He begged his mother to stop working at a school for such poor pay. He convinced her that, with adult sons, there was no need to devote so much time and energy to a difficult job like teaching. Mother resisted for a long time, arguing:

"But what about the students at the school? They got to know me so well. And there are not enough staff. How can I just drop everything and leave?"

"Mother, your health is more important to us. Last winter you caught a bad cold and ended up in the hospital with double pneumonia. And even now you feel bad in the off-season and cough. You must look after yourself!"

"Okay, dear muallim," my mother finally gave in.

Jokingly, she also called Anvar her teacher.

Anvar successfully graduated from the university and went to work in the department of higher mathematics. A year later, he decided to enrol in a graduate school in St. Petersburg. He chose that city because he missed Khovar, and Gatchina is next to St. Petersburg. But my father set the condition: once you get married, then you can go. Anvar didn't take it seriously. When he realized that father Nariman was not joking, he decided to clarify:

"Who exactly should I marry? I don't have a girlfriend and I'm very busy with my maths."

"I have already found you a bride – she's good and beautiful. She's the daughter of a famous theatre and film actress. She graduated from music school. And her name is Sarvinoz."

"Oh brother! What age are we living in?" Anvar asked me with a wink.

And after a pause he added:

"Okay, father. Just so as not to offend you, I will meet her and have a chat."

A week later, a serious men's conversation took place. Mother and

Nilufar went to a parent-teacher meeting. And the three of us boys stayed at home. Under my father's stern gaze, I wanted to escape, but Anvar stopped me:

"Brother, don't go, please! You're already an adult and have the right to solve family problems with us. I will soon go to St. Petersburg to enrol in graduate school. I will live next to Khovar. And you must remain here as the eldest. I want you to understand now that the responsibility for our family falls on your shoulders.

"I'm sitting right here! And I am your elder!" Father shouted, slamming his fist on the table. "Let Ozar leave. Let's talk one on one."

"Father, I cannot and have no right to reprimand you! Mother has taught me to be polite with you. But respect must be mutual. I insist that Ozar stay. Believe me, he knows so much that you don't even suspect. I have long been independent and am responsible for my words. And as promised, I spoke with Sarvinoz. She is a very wise and sensible girl. She told me a lot."

"Well, was it something interesting?" Father asked sarcastically.

"You live between two families," Anvar answered, "and Sarvinoz's mother is a very close 'friend' of yours. She knows that you have lost interest in her, but she cannot come to terms with it. Her youngest daughter was diagnosed with cerebral palsy at birth and requires expensive treatment, but her ex-husband ran away from these hardships and does nothing to help. Her mother is persuading Sarvinoz to marry me in order to keep you close and not lose financial assistance."

"That is none of your business," the father snapped rudely. "Who I live with and how is none of your concern."

"Father, we are having an unpleasant conversation, I understand that. But Sarvinoz herself admitted that she doesn't want to marry me, because she has a lover. Her mother doesn't like the guy though. It seems to me, that the equation isn't working out on either side. We need to look for the right solution. And frankly, after observing your attitude towards mother and towards us, I don't really feel like getting married at all."

I was very scared. Dad was beside us, seething with anger. Breathing heavily, he began to tap some strange rhythm on the table with his fingers and pierced us with his gaze, like lightning. But Anvar did not lower his eyes. And then father decided to 'justify his actions':

"What a fool, and you believed her? Sarvinoz is clearly bad-mouthing me so that she could marry that lazy musician of hers. Yes, I'm helping her mother. Doing a good deed is commanded from above."

"Father, calm down! I don't care who Sarvinoz loves. But she said she would cut her wrists if they forced her to marry me. And these kinds of thoughts are already troubling enough for all of us. For me, everything is just as clear as two by two being four. A good deed, dad, is not done in exchange for any services. I made an agreement with Sarvinoz and I will help her mother and sister. As for you, the money you give to their family would be much better spent on our mother. And for Khovar's child, because you will soon be a grandfather. It turns out that you will have to answer for everything not only in this life, but also in the future."

"Are you done? Now you listen to me, you philosopher-mathematician," said father, restraining his anger. "Mother and I will figure out our relationship ourselves. A wife must endure everything, it's not for you to set the laws here. Wherever and whoever I am with, I always return home. I am a man! And that's it! No one has ever felt bad because of me."

"No one, you say? What about Aunt Parvin? And Halima Akhmadovna? Ah... I shouldn't be naming everyone now, otherwise we'll be here for hours. It's convenient for you to live like this. Well, whatever the case, we won't interfere. Mother loved you, believed that everything would work out, endured and withstood everything for our sake. She was left with emptiness instead of love. If Khovar were nearby, he would say in the words of his revered Remarque: "The strongest feeling is disappointment. Not resentment, not jealousy or even hatred... after those, at least something remains in the soul, after disappointment, there is only emptiness."

"And where is Khovar and his Remarque now? He could have become a diplomat. But instead, he became a drunkard who ran away from his home to somewhere in the cold. Does he think a foreign land will warm him?"

"Father, it's as if you are talking about a stranger. In everything that happened, you must understand there is some fault of yours as well. If you had thought about your children first and then about others, everything could have been different," Anvar answered calmly. "Ozar would be the one giving the money to help the Sarvinoz family. Even if I did marry her, it would still be like that. That was our little knight to checkmate! An easy way to shoot down two birds with one stone!"

"Well, look at you, what a saint! Are you trying to teach me a lesson? Why are you doing this? Are you trying to disgrace your father? Every man has his own secrets. Are you trying to expose my 'sins' or whatever?"

"Dad, you would have still stopped helping that family. Because you don't tolerate anyone being around you for too long. And you put yourself and your desires above everyone and everything. As Sarvinoz said apologetically, you don't love anyone but yourself. It turns out she's right, isn't she?"

"That's it, I don't want to hear another thing out of your mouth! Shut up! You bear my last name, eat my bread, live in my house and you dare and try to teach me?! Ungrateful bastard!" Angry tears filled my father's eyes.

He waved his hand at Anvar, as if pushing him away, and muttered through his teeth:

"I have lost my second son too..."

He got up from the table and slowly walked towards the door. He thought we would stop him, but we remained silent...

This conversation was a revelation for me. I never thought that my taciturn brother would dare to reason with our father. Now I understood that Anvar is the main core of our seemingly prosperous family. Both a moral and material core.

Before leaving, Anvar gave me instructions about his workshop. Everything there was perfectly organized. He himself started his entrepreneurial activity as a schoolboy and now believed that I, with my abilities, could take over in his place. I thought it would be good work and life experience.

After that frank conversation, my father came home late and did not communicate with anyone. When my mother asked what happened, he answered that he was tired from work.

A week later Anvar left for St. Petersburg. Mother gave him a lot of gifts for Khovar and Vera, but also lots of warm clothes for Anvar himself - she knitted them herself from sheep's wool. She prepared a dowry for her first grandson.

During all three years of Anvar's graduate studies, our mother and anyone else who travelled to St. Petersburg from Zarnisor gave parcels to him and Khovar's family. One day, a student of our mother, Zarrina, now a graduate of the university's Faculty of Economics, was setting off for St. Petersburg.

We had seen that since early school she always looked at Anvar with loving eyes and blushed when they met. Mother prayed that Anvar would pay attention to this wonderful girl. Friendly meetings in St. Petersburg helped them get closer, and then understand how dear they both were to each other. It's strange, but my father was happy about this too. The now aged grandmother Salima and our aunts began to visit us again often in anticipation of the imminent wedding. Zarrina and Nilufar became friends and we all rallied around our mother.

Zarrina was the daughter of the head of customs on the Tajik-Uzbek border. And her mother was in charge of the kindergarten where Aunt Parvin once worked. Her parents were happy with their daughter's choice. They were proud that Zarrina was marrying the son of muallima Sadbarg Umarovna.

Everyone in the town was waiting for a magnificent wedding. But the newlyweds decided to have only a family evening with their relatives and hold a nikoh (wedding) ceremony at home, spending the rest of the money on expenses for arranging life in St. Petersburg. Anvar said that there was a whole life ahead of them and there would be many reasons to gather for celebrations. And the law now banned overly lavish weddings. Our mathematician decided to use this as an excuse to spend his money wisely instead.

The bride's side agreed with this. But father Nariman was categorically against it. But my brother eventually convinced him too. Father still insisted on organizing pilaf for the neighbours of our street and the wedding in the mosque.

Grandmother did not want to come to terms with this. She demanded the observance of an ancient ritual in order to ask Bibi Mushkilkusho, the lady of problem-solving, for support and blessing, before the engagement, ceremonial-crowning and all the pre-wedding events. And then, of course, would come the solemn wedding itself.

"This is the first wedding in your family," she told father. "Make sure everyone remembers this event for a long time."

But Anvar arrived and cancelled everything. He handed grandmother Salima money and asked her to perform the Mushkilkusho ritual at home, saying that God would hear her prayers anywhere. Our father was very offended at this and began to drink heavily in the evening. This could have ended in a scandal, but Anvar managed to convince his father and grandmother and accompanied them to Dushanbe. Mother did not dissuade Anvar and repeated endlessly:

"The most important thing is to be happy!"

Khovar arrived with Vera and his son Daniyar. Nilufar would not let go of the baby, kissing him and rejoicing as if it were her own son. Mother was very happy. Verajon and Zarrina helped her with the housework. Vera had liked Zarrina ever since they met in St. Petersburg. And the fact that Anvar was able to see his future with Zarrina was also a good sign.

Sarvinoz and her husband Rahim also came to congratulate the newlyweds. They filled our house with music, performing the famous song 'Mukhabbat' from the movie 'It's Time for My Son to Get Married.' Rahim played the guitar, Sarvinoz sung, and everyone gathered around and sang along in unison.

Our little sister Nilufar was in seventh heaven: everything here reminded her of her childhood! And there were even more of us. She spun around in a dance, hugging Daniyar close to her and, probably, dreamt of bringing us all together to her own wedding someday. No one could have thought on that day that Nilufar's future happiness would be cut short by fate itself…

# CHAPTER FIVE:

# Nilufar

My beloved sister was one of those children who are called angels for their kindness. Calm, bright, taciturn and grateful. She knew how to listen and her blue eyes reflected a whole range of feelings. Even if she didn't agree with something, she never argued or interrupted, and expressed her opinions with a sweet and gentle smile.

Nilufar's meek character and benevolence did not give her any urge to raise her voice or reproach anyone for anything. We are the same age and grew up together. As children, the three of us, including Ravshan, were always playing. I noticed how happy Nilufar and Ravshan were together at every gathering and could not understand why their love for each other worried Aunt Parvin. Only after her suicide and from her posthumous letter did it become clear how afraid she was of the sprouts of this early childhood love. I remember that freeze-frame of Ravshan's farewell to Uzbekistan and our farewell to him. He hesitated to get into the minibus and kept looking around, as if he was waiting for someone. And, hearing the cry of Nilufar running towards him, he rushed towards her.

"Ravshan, don't leave! How can I live without you?" Nilufar repeated, sobbing.

And he stroked his friend's head and said words that were incomprehensible to her:

"Goodbye, Jonam, this is how it's supposed to be. After all, you and I are brother and sister..."

Nilufar never learned the truth. I couldn't hurt her, so I kept silent. It seems to me that this trace of first love remained in my sister's heart forever...

One day we were sitting on the veranda and pestered our mother with questions about our names.

"Mummy, the name Sadbarg suits you so well," Nilufar said affectionately. "You are like a rose, or rather a hundred-petalled rose, and you give joy and love to everyone. Why did you choose the name you gave us? Tell me, please!"

"Well, our first one, Khovar – means the East, the side of warmth and sun," my mother answered with a smile. "Your father, the head of the family, gave his son this name. The second boy was born with such a bright smile that we immediately named him Anvar – meaning 'radiant light'. After that, I was already looking forward to my third son," my mother pointed her eyes at me. "However, I ended up carrying him with difficulty, but in end, he was born turned out to be Ozar, which means 'help from the divine light.' And just then, the nurses and doctors at the maternity hospital saw my white-skinned girl come after and gasped: "She looks like a lily!"

They said, and that's how my daughter Nilufar came to be"

Mother pressed our heads to her chest, and we, vying with each other, began to kiss her hands.

A variety of species of flowers grew in our garden, but roses and white lilies delighted our family and guests the most. Mother took care of the flowers, and as Nilufar grew up, she would do the same. We, the brothers, were trusted only with watering. Nilufar tinkered with the flowers with inspiration: weeding them, replanting them, feeding them and everything else – all with a smile and quiet chants. She cut flowers delicately and did not like large flouncy bouquets; it was important for her to admire each flower in all its beauty. Sometimes she would put one rose in a low vase and sit looking at its petals. Once, Nilufar placed three branches of lilies in a narrow clay jug and blissfully inhaled their wonderful aroma. For some reason, she didn't like factory-made vases, but loved the homemade ones sculpted by local potters. Nilufar sometimes asked me to go with her to the most famous craftsman, Usto Khairullo. I watched with interest and delight as his hands transformed a shapeless piece of clay into a product of perfect beauty. She really wanted to sit down at the potter's wheel herself, but she was too shy to ask the master.

One day, she showed me decorations she made to put on the vases and delicately asked if I could show them to Usto Khairullo. I have always been the first connoisseur of my sister's art, because she hasn't let go of coloured pencils since she was four years old. Looking at the decorations, I was amazed by the graceful oriental patterns she had made in the rich shades of green and brown, which were popular in our area. I immediately told Nilufar to get ready, adding a favourite saying from my neighbour Sashka:

"Let's go! You won't get punched on the nose for asking!"

Usto Khairullo praised the decorations and promised to think about using them in the painting process. Nilufar even blushed from embarrassment, but happiness shone in her eyes. I admired my sister, and she seemed to me the most beautiful in the world. She had thick red hair down to her waist, porcelain-white skin, eyebrows fused in the middle, and a mole in the corner of her lips. And her eyes! You could see the depth of a clear blue lake in them. They said Nilufar looked like my mother's mother, our grandmother, Gulchekhra, but it was hard to see the resemblance in a black and white photograph. Nilufar was shy and lowered her eyes when she heard exclamations of admiration about her beauty.

Her favourite word was 'nagz!' – which means 'good' or even 'wonderful'. She learned to sew and embroider early. She even made dolls herself from twigs and scraps of fabric. She created outfits for both homemade and factory-made toys, and then the neighbouring girls asked their mothers to order dresses for themselves from Nilufar in the same styles.

One day, Aunt Parvin came to see my mother with her daughters Madina and Amina. She unfolded the pieces of iridescent Crepe de Chine silk and asked if she could invite Nilufar Narimanovna to be their 'cutter'. I burst out laughing, and my mother smiled contentedly:

"Ozar, call your sister and go put some tea for us. We will have women's talk here, it's not for you to listen to."

Of course, I stood in the courtyard by the open window and heard how my little sister Nilufar advised her older friends on different styles of dresses based on her drawings. Amina and Madina then demonstrated these outfits, like models from a fashion magazine, and reluctantly named her 'craftswoman'.

And so that's how it went. The neighbours began to dream that after graduating from school, Nilufar would open her own studio in the town and give the capital's seamstresses a run for their money. And my sister cherished the hope of learning to become a real fashion designer.

My brothers spoiled Nilufar with various gifts. After getting paid for the very first time, Anvar bought her a marvellously beautiful silver and turquoise set of jewellery - a necklace, earrings, a ring and a bracelet, as well as the best German 'Singer' sewing machine. I gave her gold jewellery made in our national style, and Khovar brought wonderful jewellery made of sunny amber from Kaliningrad that really complemented Nilufar's beauty. Mother put the family jewellery in her dowry. My sister could not tolerate bright and flashy colours, but green and gold suited her red hair surprisingly well. And when she carried a dish of apricots, it was a picture that could make your heart skip a beat.

My sister loved dad very much. We as brothers, were more drawn to our mother, and she, to our father. Every day she looked forward to daddy's return from work and was happy when he picked her up from kindergarten or school. And if dad Nariman occasionally took his daughter in his arms, her happiness knew no bounds. Mother was glad that father was at least affectionate with Nilufar. She was upset when he left her daughter unattended and then she tenderly hugged and kissed her – she was the connecting thread between our parents.

Now, as an adult, I understand a lot. With the birth of his daughter, it became clear to father that there are also women who do not owe him anything, but instead, he owes them. Apparently, he couldn't accept this. Nilufar was jokingly called "hudkhur" – meaning a person who beats themselves up over things. She sincerely worried about everyone, tried to help everyone and carried other people's pain within herself. Her mother taught her daughter that it was impossible to embrace the whole world and that she should try and help without sacrificing her own health and wellbeing. But my sister's character was formed this way, and it was impossible to change her.

Nilufar was finishing school, and I was already studying at the philological department of the Tajik University and was waiting for my sister in Dushanbe, because she dreamed of entering a new technological institute and becoming a professional women's clothing designer. My mother and I discussed this more than once; she wanted Nilufar to live in the capital under my supervision. But it turned out that my father had other plans. After the school prom, my mother started talking about Nilufar's further studies, but father abruptly cut her off:

"Such a beauty cannot be allowed to leave home before marriage! We have a medical school in our city, let her go there. And you can sew dresses in your free time. Trying to do it as a profession is pointless anyway!"

Nilufar pleadingly looked at her father in silence, her eyes ready to fill with tears. And my mother tried to challenge the verdict of the head of the family:

"Anyone can be a nurse, and our daughter is very talented. She needs to develop that talent."

"It will be as I said!" Father raised his voice. "If she gets married, I'll let you go wherever you want."

Obediently, my sister obeyed the order. But she only studied at medical school for a year. As soon as she turned eighteen, match-makers began to frequent our house. Father refused everyone, considering the locals unworthy to become related to him - the Rais. And then he said that he himself had found a groom in Dushanbe - the son of a retired general. And he told everyone to prepare for the wedding. Mother tried to explain to the head of the family and begged him not to rush to give his daughter to someone else's house. But father didn't even consider it necessary to entertain her arguments. Nilufar was shocked. She timidly asked her father:

"Do you want to marry me off to a man I've never seen? I would at least like to know more about the groom, in case I don't like him..."

The father smiled sceptically:

"General Khodzhaev is my old friend, he has a good, decent family. His son's name is Khurshed and, most importantly, I like him."

Mother did not dare to get in the way of her husband's decision any longer and began to cry quietly. And father, revelling in power, looked at her as if there was nothing there. At that moment he looked so much like Grandma Salima! Nilufar felt like her mother was afraid of her father's anger and there was no one to stand up for her, because we, our sons, were not around.

And submissively bowing her head, she said in a barely audible voice:

"Okay, dad. I agree."

She put her arm around her mother's shoulders and led her into the bedroom. Then my sister told me that she and mother had been whispering all night. Nilufar hoped that she would meet the kindest person who would tell her how to build proper family relationships and be at least a little bit happy as a woman.

Mother asked me to find out more about the groom's family in Dushanbe. Among my classmates were the general's neighbours and, to be honest, the things that I heard from them worried me.

General Rafik Nizamovich Khodzhaev was well over sixty. He left his first wife and three children for a young nurse, Shodigul. It was rumoured that she was known as a lively girl and was 'systematically' looking for someone who would offer her legal marriage and look after her. It turned out that many of the gentlemen she knew were rich and high up, including our father, Nariman, who she had been pursuing for a long time. But he, naturally, had no intention of marrying her. General Khodzhaev, though, fell head over heels for the girl, although he was old enough to be her father. They met in the hospital where Khodzhaev was being treated for pneumonia, and the nurse simply bewitched him. Shodigul lived up to her name in translation - a joyful flower. She was always flirting and smiling, affectionate and attentive, and spoke sweetly and melodiously. She addressed everyone as 'jons' – meaning dearest. They say: 'Az dahonash asal mechakad' about such people, meaning someone who has 'honey dripping from their mouth.'

Khodzhaev and Shodigul never had their own children but took a boy from the orphanage instead. They named him Khurshed and raised him like a prince, pampering him and indulging him in everything. Shodigul considered all her son's peers unworthy and did not allow him to play with them, much less be friends. Both at school and at the Polytechnic Institute, Khurshed was known as a narcissistic and arrogant loner.

As you can understand, I could not share these details with my mother, and told her about the Khodzhaev family only in general terms.

On the day of the engagement, the groom and his parents actually showed up at our house. Khurshed was painfully thin, pale, with indifferent, empty eyes. He was smartly dressed, but still looked a mess. He didn't say a word all evening. You'd never even guess he was getting married. The fat, old General sat next to his wife, placing his hand on her knee in a proprietary manner. And Shodigul looked teasingly at our father Nariman, and in a melodiously sweet voice described the heavenly future life of the young couple.

Mother didn't like Khurshed at all. She could not imagine her beloved Nilufar next to this gloomy lone wolf. But our sister disarmed her with the words:

"Mummy, beauty and charm are important for women. As for men, they must be courageous. Maybe he's a good person? For some reason, I just feel sorry for him..."

It was clear that the obedient and responsive daughter accepted her father's choice and trusted him.

The groom's parents began to suggest where and how to hold the wedding. The General, although retired, stated anxiously that the republic was once again restless. He remembered with sadness how nationalistic unrest in the early 90's resulted in a civil fratricidal war, which brought a lot of grief. It took many years to restore peace and order. But even now there are those in various government structures who are dissatisfied, and it seems that the division of power will begin again very soon.

"We need to inform Khovar and Anvar about the wedding," my mother said excitedly, looking pleadingly at father.

But he waved her away with annoyance, as if she was an annoying fly: "Are you not listening, there is unrest in the republic! Do we really need to bother our sons in such an alarming situation? God forbid they get stuck here. We will have a modest wedding, without any out-of-town guests. And after that – we'll see. Once Nilufar gives birth to a child, then we can call over the rest of the relatives."

It hurt me to look at my mother and sister. It was clear that father wanted to decide his daughter's future without the interference of his obstinate sons. I'm certainly not a hindrance to him, but if Anvar and Khovar had been there, everything might have turned out differently. This is not the wedding my sister Nilufar dreamed of – not the joyful celebration she hoped for. Father Nariman hastened to 'give away' his daughter. This wedding was like Nilufar being expelled from her home. Mother walked around lost and hid her tear-stained eyes. And my father commanded us not to bother the Khodzhaev family with our visits – after all, they say that young couples need to get used to family life. Mother visited Nilufar once a month, but while I was studying in Dushanbe, I tried to see my sister more often. The General almost constantly lived at his dacha, and Shodigul lived with the young couple. When we met, I didn't recognize my sister - it was as if she was a candle that had faded after her marriage. There were no traces left of her former smile, the sparkles in her eyes, or the cheerfulness. I noticed that Nilufar began to wear dresses with long sleeves, as if hiding her delicate white skin.

One day Nilufar called the faculty dean's office and asked for me to come urgently. I took time off from my lectures and rushed to the Khodzhaev's house. I saw my sister and her mother-in-law in the yard. Shodigul stood with her back to me and this time a stream of abuse poured out of her sweet-tongued mouth. Nilufar, huddled, sat on the ground and tried to clean a large cauldron covered in soot with sand.

"Lazy! Dirty girl!" The screech rung out as I entered the gate. "Nariman was right in saying that your mother raised you to be a princess. I will teach you about life! Did you think that you could marry the General's son and get all our wealth? No, no, no! You must endure and please us, then maybe you will get a little something. Understood?"

"I don't need anything from you, just let me go home," Nilufar asked without raising her eyes.

"Don't argue with me, or I'll put you in your place so quickly that you won't even have time to blink!" The mother-in-law shouted and bent over for a stick.

I rushed over to my sister. Seeing me, Shodigul straightened up and stroked her lower back as if nothing had happened, then smiling sweetly, she said:

"Ozardjon, hello! I didn't even hear you enter the yard."

Nilufar rose to meet me and then... suddenly lost consciousness. I quickly picked her up, carried her into the house, and laid her on the bed. I called an ambulance as fast as I could. Shodigul had not expected that I would witness such a scandal and tried her best to smooth it over. While we were waiting for the doctor to arrive, Shodigul repeated in an ingratiating voice that her daughter-in-law did not do her housework well, didn't do anything on time and always wanted to go and see her mother.

"My sister is not a 'mother's girl', she is not a princess," I objected. "She is not afraid of work. Our house is larger than yours and Nilufar cleaned it alone and managed to do everything just fine. Do you need a housekeeper or daughter-in-law? Before her, who did all the housework?"

"Ozardjon, don't talk to your elders like that! I don't have to tell you anything."

"Where is Khurshed? Why doesn't he help Nilufar? I know that he is only listed as a student at the Polytechnic Institute, our building is located next to his department, but I have never seen him among my fellow students."

"That's none of your business – to know where Khurshed is. He is the General's son, jonam."

At this time, an ambulance arrived at the gate and I went out to meet the doctors. Nilufar came to her senses, but after examination, the doctor ordered her to be taken to the hospital.

"Hurry up, the patient is in danger of having a miscarriage."

"What miscarriage?" I was scared.

"She could lose the child!"

I was sitting in the ambulance next to the stretcher on which Nilufar, white as chalk, was lying, I held her hand tightly. I lifted the sleeve of her dress and saw terrible bruises and cuts on her delicate skin. I started asking who was beating her? My sister opened her exhausted eyes and whispered:

"Ozar, I just fell, my head was spinning..."

It was only a short distance to the hospital. Suddenly, Nilufar screamed, and I saw a bloody stain on the stretcher...

After losing the child, I took Nilufar from the hospital and took her home to Zarnisor. She needed to regain her strength. She lived with us for a whole month, but neither Khurshed nor his parents came to visit her. But in Dushanbe they complained about her to our dad Nariman.

My mother and I tried to find out from our dear Nilufar what she was hiding, but my sister was silent.

One day my father came home early from work and ordered his daughter:

"Get ready, I'll take you home."

"My home is here, dad," Nilufar said with a prayer in her voice.

"Have pity on your daughter! At least have Khurshed come for her," my mother interceded.

"Who is asking you? Our daughter is disgracing us. Is this thanks to your upbringing? A wife must live in her husband's house. This is the law! To endure and please! You're not getting away from this duty," father continued angrily.

"I had nowhere to go before. Now that my sons are adults, I'll go to them," mother answered through tears.

"Who even needs you? Everyone should live in their own home."

"Even if it's unbearable?"

Father did not consider it necessary to answer and turned to Nilufar:

"Go pack your things, I said! Or will you get into the car in your housedress? I've been waiting a month for you to ask me to return you to your husband."

"I'll get ready now," Nilufar answered obediently.

"I'll go with you too," I said.

"Where are you going? Khurshed's parents asked that you not come to their house anymore. Understood?"

My father didn't even spare me a glance. But I didn't give up:

"So that there will be no one to protect Nilufar? Is that what they want?"

"Protect her from who? Khurshed is completely exhausted from worry. Her mother-in-law wouldn't even hurt a fly, I know Shodigul well. The way she talks to people is something everyone could learn from," my father said in my mother's direction.

Mother couldn't stand it and, holding back tears, said with pain:

"How much crueller can you be towards your only daughter!"

Nilufar changed her clothes and having collected her things and her mother's gifts in a bundle, slowly walked to the car. She said goodbye to us with a sad smile:

"Mummy, Ozar, there is no need to worry, I'm already stronger, everything is fine. Thank you! I can handle the housework now."

I can imagine how humiliating it was for her to return to that alien family, and our father allowed her to experience such humiliation...

But I did not leave my sister to suffer, I visited her, despite the prohibitions. She let me know when no one was home. She rejoiced at my arrival like a child. She was proud that I was graduating with honours.

Mother also visited Nilufar, and on those days, everyone would leave the house, as if emphasizing their reluctance to see such a guest. Of course, it was unpleasant, but mother was willing to endure everything just to be with her daughter. I was glad no one interfered with their conversations. Sometimes I joined them.

Nilufar became pregnant two more times, but both times there was a miscarriage. And Khurshed became like a skeleton covered in skin. Mother once noticed that there was a syringe next to the trash can. She picked it up with a napkin, walked up to her daughter and asked:

"Is someone sick here? Who is getting injections?"

Nilufar was scared. And mother continued:

"Don't be silent, otherwise I'll take the syringe and hand it over for examination."

"No need, mother, I'll tell you everything. I didn't want to upset you with my problems. Khurshed is a drug addict. That's why he's so skinny. He recently had withdrawal symptoms. Mother-in-law was forced to call a doctor. I heard their conversation. The doctor insisted on Khurshed's hospitalization. Otherwise, he won't last long."

"That's why you don't wear jewellery. Did he sell everything to buy drugs? That's why things don't work out for you with children. Why are you putting up with all this?"

"Mother, sometimes I really do feel sorry for him. When there are bright spots, he reveals his wounded soul. He is afraid of his mother, and his father does not fight for him. My mother-in-law stopped tormenting me because I don't leave Khurshed and don't disgrace them. All of the neighbours sympathize with me, after all, you can't cover the sun with a hem. I must carry this burden. Khurshed's parents constantly take him to the dacha. My mother-in-law would irritability say: "A stranger – he's nothing but a stranger." And for Khurshed, those bright spots are becoming less and less frequent. He can be scary when he demands drugs. Only God knows how tired I am of all this. But I don't want to burden anyone with my problems. I have come to terms with it."

"Get ready, we're going home to Zarnisor," my mother said decisively. "I have one daughter. Stop putting up with these humiliations."

"I would have left long ago, but I'm afraid of father. How many times will he bring me back? And it's not easy for you. I am between not two, but three fires."

"But father will now know the reason and will not allow you to live with a drug addict."

"Father knows everything, Mummy."

"How can that be? He knew everything and left you to be torn to pieces? Why did your father decide to punish you like this? Or me?"

Nilufar began to cry, and so did mother. I even got a headache from what I heard and from pity for my family. But I had to behave like a man, and I strictly demanded that my sister pack her things. I called a taxi and we left. On the way, I remembered the lines from Aunt Parvin's letter:

*"Dear Sadbarg, I know that many will judge me. They will say that you must be strong, think about the children. I lived with this burden for ten years and constantly wanted to erase the terrible memories of that night from my mind. Is it possible to fight on a battlefield where everything is subject to patriarchal canons and people that depend on public opinion, which in most cases is subjective? I pray to God that no one will ever be in my place..."*

I looked at Nilufar and thought, she was supposed to be happy. And my sister could also not resist the unwritten laws of our imperfect society. She was afraid of publicity and gossip.

We arrived home late and, tired, went straight to bed. In the morning, father found out that Nilufar was at home. He waited until everyone had gathered for breakfast and carried out his interrogation:

"You came here again without asking your husband's permission?"

"But her husband was high and didn't care," I immediately came up with an excuse for my sister.

"I'm not asking you," the father barked.

"I miss my family very much," Nilufar answered quietly.

"You better go back today!"

"Okay, dad. I'll be gone by the end of the day."

Nilufar's answer sounded somewhat defeated, but I thought about her eternal humility and did not draw out anymore conflict.

Father went to work. Mother began to bustle around in the kitchen, preparing Nilufar's favourite dish - dumplings. Our faithful neighbour, Aunt Anora, came to her aid. I went to the garden to collect fruit for dinner, and Nilufar decided to clean my mother's room.

In the garden I noticed a drooping lily; its stem was broken. I suddenly felt uneasy. A bad feeling, creeping from our home, crawled through every fibre of my being. Nilufar lay on her mother's bed, calm and peaceful. And on the floor lay an empty bottle of my mother's sleeping pills. Nilufar was gone.

Brother Khovar and Anvar came to say goodbye to their sister. We buried Nilufar next to Aunt Parvin. Before our eyes, my mother turned black with grief and kept repeating that she could not save her beautiful lily, her daughter from death.

We, her sons, decided to leave Zarnisor and take our mother with us. They understood that it was a bad idea to leave her with father Nariman...

## CHAPTER SIX:

# Grandmother Gulchekhra

My mother's mother, Gulchekhra, died during childbirth, and grandfather, Umar Anvarov, spoke sparingly about her. I will try to restore the fate of my grandparents as retold by their daughter Sadbarg.

Umar and Gulchekhra lived next door in the city of Hoit. Their families were friends and their parents were happy that each of their own children entered the correspondence department of the Dushanbe Pedagogical Institute almost simultaneously. They began to work in their native Hoit school - Gulchekhra taught native language and literature, Umar taught mathematics. Both were considered the best teachers in the region and were often invited to the capital for republican seminars. Relatives noticed that Gulchekhra and Umar sympathized with each other but did not rush things and waited until the young couple confessed their feelings to one another. The neighbours were already talking about the wedding. But a formidable element wiped out both the city and the people from the face of the earth. Umar and Gulchekhra were in the capital, at the Ministry of Education, at that time.

I learned about the tragic event later from the press during perestroika, because previously such information was classified in the Union. Here is an excerpt from that newspaper publication:

"Early in the morning of July 10th, 1949, in the year of the 20th anniversary of the formation of the Tajik SSR, one of the largest natural disasters in the history of the USSR occurred - the earthquake in Hoit. The city of Hoit in the Hoit district (now the Tajikabad district) of the Khatlon region of Tajikistan was once a busy settlement with a bustling bazaar, mosques and a caravanserai. Khait was located 190 km from Dushanbe. More than 60 thousand people lived in this area. In just a matter of seconds, absolutely nothing remained of the city and the surrounding areas. Hoit was enveloped in a thick column of dust, the sky was clouded with darkness. Under a deafening, growing roar, a 100-meter-long mass rapidly approached the city. One by one, houses turned into ruins, burying people underneath them. Many ran in different directions in horror, but the terrible force of the shocks threw people up and overturned them as if into the underworld. At the same time, huge masses of stone rushed towards Hoit from different directions at terrifying speed."

On that terrible day, Umar and Gulchekhra lost all their relatives. Both realized that fate had left them alive for a reason and that they must move on together. A year later they had a modest wedding. They graduated from the pedagogical institute with honours. According to mother's stories, her parents, who suffered from the natural disaster, were first provided with a dormitory, and then with a one-room apartment in a new building. Umar and Gulchekhra lived in perfect harmony. They worked as teachers at an orphanage. And they themselves were preparing to become parents.

In January 1952, Umar took his wife to the maternity hospital and stood guard outside the windows, waiting for news of the birth of their child. The nurse showed him his daughter briefly, and then the doctor came out and said that the birth was difficult and Gulchekhra could not be saved. Umar was struck as if by thunder. For a long-time he could not come to his senses and remembered the earthquake in his native Hoit, which spared his beloved. How they both dreamed that they would have a long and happy life, many children and joy in the house. And now the earth covered Gulchekhra and her final resting place was a grave in the cemetery.

The orphanage nurses called the newborn girl a 'rose' and fed her from a bottle, put her to bed and walked with her while Umar was teaching in class. In the evening, Umar brought his daughter to their one-room apartment and, looking at her face, reproached himself for not feeling much love for the child. It seemed that fate had broken him and nothing, not even little Sadbarg, could save him from the storm of life.

Compassionate fellow teachers in the orphanage noticed how a young woman, Dilnoza, an assistant cook in the kitchen, was staring at Umar. She lived in the next building to Umar, and somehow naturally became a helper both with the baby and in his house. Umar had a hard time getting used to Dilnoza, but in the end he realized that he couldn't raise his daughter alone. This is how a new family was created and Sadbarg began to grow up with her stepmother.

Soon Dilnoza became pregnant and gave birth to a son. She left work because her maternity leave never ended – she gave birth to two more sons and two daughters who were born one after another. The expanded family now lived in Dilnoza's large apartment, and Umar wrote a 'deed of gift' to his daughter Sadbarg for the previous one-room apartment. It was as if he felt that the girl would remain an orphan.

My mother said that she remembers herself from the age of five. She called Dilnoza mother, but Dilnoza only looked kindly at her stepdaughter in front of her husband, but when he wasn't around, she endlessly hissed angrily at the baby. When Sadbarg grew up, she became a nanny for her brothers and sisters.

In school, teachers couldn't get enough of Sadbarg at first, but then they began to notice that the girl came to class tired and would drift to sleep during class. Her father was called in for a conversation, and Umar admitted that his daughter was the main assistant in their large family. His salary as a teacher was not enough and he had to change his profession. At the insistence of his wife, he became a truck driver and was constantly on the road. The class teacher then said:

"Sadbarg is a very capable and talented girl. It would be a pity if she started skipping lessons and not studying to her full potential. I understand that it's not easy for her at home, but what kind of future are you, her father, preparing for your daughter? Do you want her to go to university and get a profession? Or will she be left as a nanny for the rest of her life?"

After that conversation, Umar's mind would drift off during work, and he kept thinking and thinking about the fate of his daughter. Once, returning from a long drive, he decided to talk to Sadbarg. Our mother told us many times about that conversation in the park near our house. Retracing exactly how the conversation went:

"Daughter, I know it's very difficult for you. I would like you to study more. You are already 14 years old, it's time to think about your future profession and university. You don't and never will have time at home with your brothers and sisters. Your mother, Gulchekhra, is seeing everything from heaven. She will not forgive me, knowing that my daughter abandoned her studies for the sake of household chores. Let me take you to the orphanage where my mother and I worked, what do you say?"

"I promise that I will keep up, daddy. I just want to be close to you."

"How will you ever find the time? You are like Cinderella here, you have work fit for ten people. When I'm around, I see you don't have even a minute for yourself. And I don't even want to imagine how it is when I'm off driving. It will be more comfortable in the orphanage. Don't be upset about this decision. I will visit you and take you home during the weekends.

Then the father unfolded an old silk scarf, and sorrowfully said:

"Sadbarg, I'll give you letters and photographs of your mother. I put them away so that they wouldn't catch my eye and poison my soul. As if you can hide a memory... Believe me, I loved your mother Gulchekhra very much and I still can't forget her. For a long time, I even considered you guilty of her death. Forgive me, daughter!

Your mother gave you life, and she left us... I thought you would be like her, but Gulchekhra gave you only her character - calmness and patience. Your mother was of unusual beauty – she was white-skinned, with fiery red hair. I never tired of admiring her and even, jealously, was proud when I heard the melodious compliments, 'burning-golden curls' and 'blue eyes.' I really want you to continue your teaching profession just like your mother."

Our mother recalled this with tears in her eyes. I don't know why, but I imagined that the women from my mother's side of the family were cursed by some evil curse. Grandmother Gulchekhra lived a short life and died during childbirth, her daughter Sadbarg and granddaughter Nilufar suffered and became victims of family relationships and domestic violence. But the Eastern wisdom: "Sometimes fate is written with our own hands," is also true. It isn't wars, natural disasters, nor circumstances that break a person, but they themselves chooses the path of war or peace for themselves and their loved ones. None of us should forget that mercy is greater than hatred.

...Before final exams, her father stopped visiting Sadbarg. She was very worried but thought that maybe dad didn't want to distract her. Two weeks passed quickly, but her father never came. After presenting the certificate, the director called Sadbarg to his office and conveyed the sad news. Umar Anvarov did not return from his last drive because his truck had been caught in a rockfall on the pass and fell into a deep abyss. Her father was dead. Sadbarg ran to her brothers and sisters, but her stepmother would not let her into the house. She screamed on the threshold that Sadbarg was to blame for everything.

Then Dilnoza moved with her children to another city without leaving an address. The rest of the relatives just shrugged and remained silent. Sadbarg looked for a family for a long time, because apart from her half-brothers and sisters, she had no relatives. But no matter how hard she searched, there was no one. All she had was her parents' apartment – and photographs, books and letters from grandmother Gulchekhra, tied with a green silk ribbon. From them, our mother Sadbarg learned a lot about the life of our grandmother. She carefully kept all these things in a gilded box, as the only memories of her past.

I will give only two excerpts from grandmother Gulchekhra's notes:

*"My dear Umar! I hope that we and our children will read these notes of mine someday together and remember how God saved the two of us from the earthquake. Probably, we were left so that the memory of our fellow countrymen would not go away along with that beautiful valley among the mountains, swallowed up overnight. We must live! I believe in our destiny to be bearers of the memory of our relatives, loved ones, and neighbours. I wish I could live to old age..."*

Mother always cried reading these lines and repeated:

"It turns out that God saved mother Gulchekhra only for my birth."

"Thank God he saved her! Otherwise, we, your children, would not exist," I reassured my mother, wiping her tears.

In the last part of the notes, our grandmother addressed her unborn child:

*"Soon you will be born, my joy. I don't know if you're a boy or a girl. If you're a boy, I want you to become Rustam, a real legendary hero and be healthy and live for many years. If you are a girl, I want you to be Sadbarg - a hundred-petalled rose in a beautiful flower basket, arousing admiration for its uniqueness. I am waiting for your birth, my future child. I imagine how I will swaddle you, feed you, teach you to speak, and see your first steps. You will have many brothers and sisters. I promise! You are the first fruit of our love and you will be happy. I believe that with your arrival the house will be filled with happiness, laughter, joy..."*

Father Nariman hated it when my mother read Grandma Gulchekhra's notes. One day he came back drunk and threatened to burn them. Mother hid the letters and photos away, and I never did find them. It's a real pity! I could have used the rest of grandma Gulchekhra's notes in my Book of Life.

## CHAPTER SEVEN:

# My beloved mother Sadbarg

"You don't choose your relatives," my mother would often repeat when me and my siblings quarrelled or were offended at each other.

And she also added:

"My dears, remember you are not alone. And after you, will come the long 'tail' of our Qurboni descendants as well. It's such a joyous thought! Hold on to each other and let your children grow up as friends. You are luckier than me. My mother Gulchekhra died during childbirth and did not even have time to see her little baby. I had to grow up with my stepmother and stepbrothers and sisters, and then in an orphanage. When dad Umar died in a rockfall whilst driving, I thought of supporting our family, but my stepmother left, leaving me no address and no hope of ever meeting my family. And God loves all his children - both righteous and sinners. He gave me and you the great joy of living in a large family with numerous relatives. This is the greatest wealth!"

It is hard for me to write about my mother, although I remember keenly the priceless moments of our communication. Of her four children, I was with my mother the longest - both in joy and in sadness. Maybe that's why I became so sentimental, unlike my brothers. And I was the only one who inherited my mother's profession of philology. I grew up listening to her stories about the life and work of poets and listened with excitement as my mother read poems and excerpts from Tajik-Persian prose.

And oh, how many proverbs and sayings my mother knew! Her speech was figurative, she could compare our every action with heroes from folklore and literature. Each of us was the hero Rustam, the simpleton Afandi, the crazy Majnun, the merciless sorcerer-diva. And my mother also told the parables of Jalallidin Rumi on every occasion. Brother Khovar looked for similar parables and fables from other Eastern European authors, and together we tried to determine their similarities and differences.

I remember all my mother's bedtime stories, lullabies and nursery rhymes that just taught themselves to me. My friends said that their grandmothers would tell them fairy tales and sing songs. But our grandmother Salima did not do this. And she answered all our requests with a contemptuous smile:

"Your mother is a master at telling fairy tales. But I will teach you about real, not fictitious, lives, so that you can remember your roots. After all, I didn't spend all of my childhood growing up in an orphanage."

I didn't understand why my mother's shoulders sadly dropped at these words. But then I learned from Nilufar that my mother was an unloved daughter-in-law. Neither Salima's grandmother, nor her daughters Mairam and Sairam could forgive the poor orphan

Sadbarg, who, according to them, had screwed up their beloved son and brother Nariman.

Before Nilufar's sudden wedding, Nilufar's mother had sat on her daughter's bed all night, comforting her and talking about her own marriage. I thank my sister to this day for sharing our family history with me.

Fate brought Sadbarg together with the family of her future husband on the same street. An elderly couple moved into a comfortable apartment opposite hers, and Sadbarg, a student at the pedagogical institute, immediately volunteered to help her new neighbours.

That was how they met. It was clear that the head of the family, Abdullo Qurboni, was very ill and his fussy and loud wife Salima was in charge of everything. She immediately told Sadbarg that her husband was not an ordinary pensioner, but a great man who had worked for a long time as director of the Institute of Political History. They have three children: two daughters, Mairam and Sairam, who had already married and now live separately, and their son, Nariman, who was studying at higher party courses in Tashkent.

Aunt Salima very much regretted that, due to her husband's illness, they had to exchange their planned house for an apartment in a high-rise building. She liked everything about her yard, although she had to wash in the city bathhouse and use the 'medieval' toilet that was at the end of the yard. But there was air and space!

Somehow, of course, Sadbarg became Aunt Salima's main assistant in caring for the patient. After classes at the institute, she ran to the pharmacy for medicine, cleaned the rooms, and sat by uncle Abdullo's bedside, distracting him from his sad thoughts. He jokingly called Sadbarg 'a ray of light in a dark kingdom.'

And although his own daughters Mairam and Sairam came to visit their father, they behaved like guests. And their mother had little time to care for her sick husband; she was always going on about how she now had to be the main provider and earn a living.

Aunt Salima did not have a higher education and did not work anywhere, but she was always busy. She was known as Bibi-Khalifa - a reader of the Koran and a leader at traditional and ritual women's gatherings. She received money and gifts for this. She wore dresses made from the most fashionable fabrics, despite the shortages during those times. She was called nothing less than "the wife of Abdullo Qurboni" and Salima was proud of this, like a crown on her head. Her husband's merits allowed her to visit the government clinic and government store, instead of languishing in queues like a mere mortal.

The sickly uncle Abdullo sincerely believed that he was very lucky with his sweet neighbour Sadbarg. And she appreciated him for his nobility, kindness and prudence. Despite his frailness, he read a lot, shared his knowledge, was keenly interested in news and knew how to listen carefully. He also often called Sadbarg his daughter, at which Aunt Salima shook her head reproachfully and snorted with displeasure.

One day, Abdullo's doctor visited his patient at home and prescribed him a new medicine. Sadbarg volunteered to go to the pharmacy, but Aunt Salima went into the patient's room with the prescription and said:

"For how long are you going to take these pills? You know, I also constantly have pain. And you know what I use for treatment? A shot of vodka and delicious pilaf! And I immediately feel much better! And you, Abdullo, must try treating yourself according to my prescription."

Sadbarg froze, dumbfounded. But Aunt Salima was already pouring vodka into a glass, forcing her husband to drink it, and feeding him spoon by spoon with pilaf, which she herself loved more than any other dish.

The course of this 'treatment' with pilaf and vodka lasted a couple of weeks, and sometimes Uncle Abdullo even felt better. But then his liver reacted and ambulances were called more and more often.

The doctors insisted that Abdullo Qurboni needed rest, a strict diet, and constant medication. Then he was prescribed injections. Sadbarg became not only a caretaker and nanny, but also a nurse - she learned how to give injections and prepare dietary meals. She was surprised that Aunt Salima did not take her husband's illness seriously.

"What kind of disease do you have that doesn't let you eat delicious food? In my opinion, better to die with a full belly than to live according to a prescription," she repeated every now and then.

The visiting doctors advised many times that Uncle Abdullo needed to be in hospital, but his wife told them that he would be better at home. However, the disease progressed, and the sisters decided to inform Nariman about their father's critical condition. He arrived from Tashkent out of the blue. He quietly opened the door to the patient's room and saw a girl sitting by the bed. She turned towards the sound of footsteps, and Nariman was struck by the bright eyes, gentle face and shy smile. And the father, trying to get out of bed, extended his hands to his son:

"Nariman, thank Allah, you've arrived! I'm so glad to see you son! Let me hug you, dear boy!"

Nariman knelt by the bed and, clasping his father with both arms, pressed the frail man towards himself. With a lump in his throat, he felt how thin and weak his father's body had become. For all of his life Abdullo Qurboni stood out for his tall stature, powerful physique, and a handsome, noble face.

"I'm alive thanks to this angel," the frail man leaned back on the pillows and pointed to Sadbarg. "God sent her to me! Don't be embarrassed, daughter, this is the truth. You have a heart of gold and gentle hands. I have never received so much warmth, kindness and care from any of my other relatives. Thank you, dear Sadbarg!"

Aunt Salima floated into the room, followed by her daughters Mairam and Sairam.

"Sadbarg, go home, we'll sort our family matters by ourselves," Aunt Salima chirped with a wry smile, and it became clear that she had heard her sick husband's words of praise for Sadbarg. Sadbarg lowered her head and left. But before she had time to unlock her door, Nariman came up He took her hand and looked into her eyes:

"Don't be offended by my mother, I beg of you! This is how she has always been - she will make anyone dance to her tune. But father is a different person and he realized that you are a real treasure, Sadbarg! Thank you! Will I see you tomorrow?"

From these words, Sadbarg's heart trembled from embarrassment and she, lowering her head, hurried to go into her flat.

From that point on the girl devoted more time to studying at the institute and began to visit her sick neighbour less often. Nariman loved his father and looked after him better than his mother and sisters.

During these meetings at the patient's bedside, Sadbarg felt that Nariman liked her. For the first time she realized how calm and safe she felt near the stately, courteously handsome man.

And then, at the insistence of the doctors, Nariman took his father to the hospital. Abdullo did not get any better there; he slowly slipped away before their eyes and hardly spoke. He looked at his relatives who were visiting him with sad eyes and tried to smile.

One day Nariman knocked on the door of Sadbarg's apartment early in the morning and conveyed his father's request to come to the hospital. On the way, Nariman became nervous and Sadbarg was also very worried.

Aunt Salima and her daughters were already sitting in the patient's room, and all three looked back in bewilderment at Sadbarg who came in with Nariman.

"It's good that you came, daughter," Uncle Abdullo said with difficulty. "I can't imagine our family without you."

"You, too, have become like family to me," Sadbarg said quietly.

"Is everyone here? That's good," Uncle Abdullo addressed the family. "I don't have long to live. I want to say goodbye to you. I forgive everyone and ask everyone to forgive me."

Everyone tensed up. Aunt Salima felt for the first time that everything was more serious than she thought. Tears welled up in her eyes. Mairam and Sairam, pushing Sadbarg aside, rushed to their father's bed. And he continued to speak, though barely audibly:

"My dears, do not refuse my last request. I want Nariman and Sadbarg to get married. I can't imagine a better wife for my son. Think about it, my children! Please, Sadbarg, do not refuse Nariman!"

Sadbarg's eyes widened at what she heard, and she covered her flushed face with her hands. Behind her, she immediately heard Aunt Salima's angry attack:

"I don't need a daughter-in-law who is an orphan and with no dowry!

I know what kind of girls grow up in orphanages – the dissolute and overly independent!"

"Dad, why didn't you ask us?" Mairam and Sairam shouted, interrupting each other. "Is there really no other wife more worthy for our beloved brother Nariman?"

"It's not your business to arrange the fate of my son. You are the teachers of your own children, and you will teach them how to live," Uncle Abdullo calmly answered. "I want to ask you, Sadbarg, did I offend you with my decision?"

As a sign of protest, Aunt Salima began to quietly read a prayer and left the room with her daughters.

"I don't even know what to do," Sadbarg said with tears. "I hardly know Nariman..."

"The doctors said I have a few days left. Please thing about it, my dear," Uncle Abdullo urged her with a plea. "I want my only son to be happy. Of course, one cannot rush when it comes to matters such as this. But I will leave this world in peace, knowing that such a wonderful person will live by my son's side.

"Father, I will be more than glad if Sadbarg agrees," Nariman said without raising his eyes.

The words sounded like a proposal and Sadbarg, flushed with embarrassment, quietly said goodbye and left.

In the corridor she was met with the dissatisfied exclamations and glances from Aunt Salima and her daughters.

In the evening, Nariman came to Sadbarg's house for a serious conversation.

"I never thought that this is how families are created," she began.

"I don't even know how to explain it to you, Sadbarg. This is probably love at first sight. I was amazed by your kind nature and sincerity. I love and respect my father very much. He felt my attitude towards you and could not help but support me. But you can refuse if you don't want to marry me," Nariman said calmly.

"According to custom, your mother should have the final say. How do you expect to marry me without her permission and blessing? I respect Uncle Abdullo very much, but I don't know what to tell him. I feel bad for him…"

"Your consent will give peace to his soul. I don't want to insist, Sadbarg, but father is waiting for a positive answer."

"What will our life be like? I don't even really know you, and I only know about love from books. You said that you fell in love with me at first sight, but what if you only feel that way out of pity for your father and the desire to make his last moments happy? Are you ready to love me always? I have experienced so much grief and loss that I truly hope that God blesses me with happy days ahead."

"I promise that you will live in joy, we will have a big family. Don't worry about mother. She has always dreamt of a kind, intelligent and gentle-tempered daughter-in-law. I will persuade her, and she will agree with my choice."

"Let me think some more," Sadbarg asked.

The next morning Nariman came with a huge bouquet of rare hundred-petalled roses of the 'sadbarg' variety. Sadbarg had never received such gifts from anyone and, overwhelmed with gratitude, stammered, "Thank you."

"Today, father is waiting for the both of us. Let's go visit him together," Nariman asked.

"I wanted to go after class."

"Can we take time off together from the institute, just for today?"

"Alright then. I understand that every minute is precious."

At the hospital, both noticed that Abdullo Qurboni was barely breathing. He motioned for them to come closer, and with his gaze asked about the marriage proposal. Nariman looked at Sadbarg and she extended her hand to him. Abdullo Qurboni nodded his head, as if blessing the children, and then closed his eyes for the last time…

Aunt Salima treated Sadbarg calmly but coldly during the funeral and wake. Nariman, as promised, persuaded his mother to agree to his marriage. In the summer, after the last wake, they got married. Sadbarg graduated from the institute, and the young family lived in Tashkent for the last year of Nariman's studies of higher political courses. This was the happiest year of their lives.

They returned to Dushanbe and their first child, Khovar, was born. Then Nariman was sent to work in Zarnisor, where his career took off. During his time there, he changed, becoming an important official, and did not notice how he had lost his best human qualities. With every year that passed his ego grew. He came to believe himself omnipotent and able to subjugate anyone he chose to, and intrigue, flattery and sycophancy became necessary fuel for him.

Nariman often travelled to Dushanbe for meetings at the ministry and to visit his mother Salima and his sisters. It seems that he had other meetings that were 'joyful' for the soul and body. Sadbarg was already the mother of four children and had lost the former tenderness that had attracted her husband so passionately at the beginning of their lives. She began to notice her husband's coldness towards her and the children, but there was never time to find out the reasons. Sadbarg devoted herself entirely to her family and her work at school. She thanked God that she was no longer alone: she had a home, children, relatives, and greeted every new day with joy.

...The suicide of my beloved sister Nilufar devastated my mother. We often thought about her and regretted that we did not try harder to protect our delicate lily.

"I am to blame for the tragic death of my daughter," mother lamented. "Nilufar repeated my fate and lived with her husband out of pity. But family should only exist for love. We shouldn't have married our girl against her will. It turns out that we, the parents, are to blame for the unhappiness of our children."

At these moments I remembered the old woman - the mother of Halima Akhmadovna, who saw me off from her daughter's funeral with the words: "I hope that Akhriman will end up burying his daughter the same way!" How many similar curses were whispered behind our father's back? And my mother suffered the most. I tried to console her, persuaded her not to torment herself, because no one had ever managed to argue with fate.

"With my own two hands, I gave my daughter away to a man who turned out to be a drug addict and a sadist," the mother sobbed desperately. "But I could have insisted and prevented this wedding from happening. I should have gone with you, Ozar, and with Nilufar to live with your brothers, either to St. Petersburg with Anvar or to Gatchina with Khovar. There is always a way out of any situation, as long as there is hope. But our Eastern feminine tendency to be obedient, submissive and unquestioningly fulfil our husband's demands, makes us vulnerable. But a wife should not be a slave! She must be able to stand up for her little ones and think about their happiness. Grandmother Salima thinks that I live in a dream world, and that I have my head in the clouds for believing such things."

"That's right, mother," I assented. "Grandmother always says that you have risen to seventh heaven and refuse to come down."

"Maybe she's right. I've gone through a lot of grief and trials, I wanted to build a happy life for my children with my own hands. But I failed. I didn't save my girl... But you, my sons, thank God, you are alive – you are my three heroes, my three warriors!"

"I am the youngest, just like from the fairy tale - Ivan the Fool! Or Emelya the fool, right?" I tried to turn our conversation in a positive direction.

"How kind and gentle you are, Ozar!" Mother smiled through her tears. "Your adolescence passed with me and Nilufar, and we cared for you with our womanly gentleness."

I then thought about the tragic letter of revelation from Aunt Parvin, which I never showed to my mother. And I knew I couldn't show her the painful scar from the letter that ate away at me for the entirety of my childhood, the scar across my heart, inflicted by the cruel truth...

Mother was now holding on to me like a straw. And I tried to come to Zarnisor more often to be with her. I was working on my PhD thesis in comparative literature, and my mother actively helped select and analyse texts from Tajik literature. I often recited poetry and prose by heart, and I admired my mother at those moments. Her memory was extremely unique.

I remember how proud of me my mother was when I defended my dissertation. How attentively I listened to the speeches of my opponents and words of praise addressed to me. At the end, mother was also given the floor. She thanked everyone and read the poems of Abdurahman Jami:

*Khech nemat bekhtar az farzand nest.*

*Chuz ba chon farzandro payvand nest.*

*Khosil az farzand gardad komi mard.*

*Zinda az farzand monad nomi mard.*

*There is no wealth in the world richer than a child,*

*The bond that ties your souls is pure and undefiled.*

*And when you are gone, your family will live on many years,*

*They'll bring glory to your name, spreading good and cheers.*

I was very pleased that everyone present listened to my mother's speech with attention and unanimously applauded.

I managed to tell my mother that I had fallen in love with a fellow student, Gulbahor. These debates were the first time we'd seen each other, and our feelings were shown not in words, but just with looks and smiles.

Mother immediately noticed changes in my character.

"You have become stronger and more courageous, my Ozar! True love transforms a person. I will pray that you will have this feeling forever. Never listen to anyone who thinks otherwise. Through any situations in life, you must be together, trust each other. I will be waiting for you to bring your chosen one to our house. I dream of dancing at your wedding."

But my mother was not destined to meet Gulbahor. She was already seriously ill and the doctors made a disappointing diagnosis - a lung abscess.

My father almost never came home, and when he did, he was drunk. And he stubbornly 'did not notice' our mother. Even when she was in the hospital, he did not visit. But I didn't ignore her. She lovingly told me that she was glad to have such a kind and sympathetic son. My older brothers Khovar and Anvar vied with each other and offered to take my mother with them. But she was very worried about our father. She admitted to me that she had no love left for him, but only pity. She knew our father would be lost without her. And it'd be a shame for a man if his wife leaves him and his children abandon him.

In secret from us, my mother decided to have an operation, although the doctors doubted a successful outcome. In her last letter, she explained her readiness to die.

*"If I am not destined to undergo the operation, then may God take me to himself. The person to whom I gave my whole life no longer needs me. I can't bring myself to harm my body. I always thought that I was a strong woman. I endured so many adversities with dignity... Now I understand why women choose suicide. Domestic violence drives them to despair. I chose a different path. Forgive me, my children. In the event of my death, I want to be buried next to Nilufar."*

On the third day after the operation, my mother passed away. Her passing was unexpected for all of us.

Khovar and Anvar came to the funeral. Father was afraid to turn in their direction, feeling the glances full of reproach. The brothers lamented that they could not save their mother.

"God gives and God takes away. Which means that your mother's days in this world are now over," Grandma Salima reassured us in her own way.

"It wasn't her turn," Anvar answered bitterly.

"Who decides whose turn it is up there, my dear Anvar? Maybe God just wants the very best," I objected.

They put our mother in the cemetery next to the graves of Nilufar and Aunt Parvin. Almost all of Zarnisor came to see her off on her last journey. They only said good things about her. Our neighbour, Aunt Anora-kayvonu, stood close by and consoled us. I met and saw off my mother's last guests. Grandmother Samila and her entourage stood aside and didn't even cry.

Vera and Zarrina came to the first big wake (which lasts seven days). I was glad that my mother united us again. My dear Gulbahor came to help me, and I introduced her to everyone. My brothers really liked her. Gulbahor also met with Vera and Zarrina, they became friends quite quickly, despite the age difference.

Only our father, as always, was dissatisfied, because the fate of his children was being arranged without his knowledge. Did he think about the loss of his wife – the person closest to him? It's unlikely, although he understood that now it would be most difficult for him. He began to leave the house again and drank more and more often. We saw with regret that even the death of a loved one did not bring him to his senses.

Before my brothers left, I gave them my mother's farewell letter. Khovar could not read it; tears were streaming down his face. Anvar took the piece of paper and, having collected himself, calmly began to read aloud. Anvar read the last lines twice:

*"...My beloved children, remember me only with joy. Know that I will always be there. I will protect you from heaven. Do not be sad".*

## CHAPTER EIGHT:

# Grandmöther Salima

"We only live once!" was our grandmother's favourite saying. She followed the path that she 'drew up' for herself. And she taught us, her grandchildren from Zarnisor, by example. Nilufar and I felt Grandma Salima's dislike towards our mother with our childish hearts, especially her unkind attitude. Only father Nariman, her only son, was beloved in our grandmother's heart. But still, my mother never allowed either herself or us to show even a shadow of resentment or disrespect towards her.

"Love and appreciate what you have and those whom God has given you," she repeated.

Our mother felt sorry for everyone except herself.

I wrote down many facts of my grandmother's biography based on her stories, and later added my own observations.

Our grandmother Salima proudly said that she was from the family of a wealthy merchant Khoja Ibrahim Khan. They were originally from Shakhrisabz, an ancient city located near Samarkand. They lived well until the volleys of the October Revolution reached

Central Asia. During the revolution, the rich were not spared, and Salima's father decided to flee beyond the cordon with his family. At their first stop in Penjakent, he realized that it would be difficult to cross the mountains with his children. He left them and his wife in a small town and promised to pick everyone up once he had crossed and figured everything out. Salima never learned anything about fate of her father: he disappeared, cutting off all loose ends. And their bleak days of survival dragged on.

"My mother Mekhriniso got up when the roosters crowed, she would go to the mountain river in winter and summer for water, and we, her four chicks, tried to help. Our ice-cold water splashed out of buckets along the way, and we often came home wet. It was hard and cold even in the summer. We collected brushwood to somehow keep the house warm. The main food was stew. And my mother earned money by sewing - she had talent as a dressmaker. Local women brought her pieces of fabric, she cut out dresses by eye and sewed them by hand with one needle."

"Mother often looked at the road, waiting for news from our missing father. She took a deep breath so that no tears would fall, she was afraid of scaring us. At such moments we huddled close to her, hugging and warming her. I, the eldest of us, felt especially sorry for mother, realizing how difficult it was for her to raise four children alone in a foreign land. My sister, Savri, and brothers, Bekhzod and Sherzod, grew up weak and often got sick.

"During the Great Patriotic War (the Second World War), hunger, cold and deprivation took their toll. First, my sister died, and then my brothers followed. Of the four children, I was the only one left."

In Zarnisor, Nilufar and I listened to these life stories from grandmother Salima instead of fairy tales, and we were very empathetic. Nilufar was usually silent, and I was in a hurry to ask questions:

"Grandma, why were you the only one left? Was it because you were the strongest and most persistent?"

"I was the oldest, and my body was probably stronger," she answered. "Only Allah knows the answers to these questions. For some reason he needed me here."

And so Mekhriniso began to cherish her remaining precious kin like the apple of her eye.

She doted on Salima and gave the very best to her daughter. She dreamed of seeing her educated and happy. In the town, Mekhriniso was known as the best dressmaker. She made clothes for the entirety of the local 'elite'. And she tried to dress her daughter in beautiful dresses.

"Mother called me God's favourite," my grandmother proudly repeated to us. "I would walk with her to school, right up until the final exams. She 'pushed' me harder to get better grades than I might have wanted to back then, which I thank her for. She took me to different clubs. I sang beautifully, danced, and played table tennis."

Once Nilufar timidly asked her grandmother to tell us about her acquaintance with Abdullo Qurboni, our grandfather.

"That's a different story," she pretended to sigh. "For me, everything was decided in one day. Not everyone will be so lucky!"

We listened with our mouths open, as we learned that young Salima, after graduating from school, left her mother alone for the first time and went straight to the capital - the city of Dushanbe, deciding to enter the economics department of the university.

Mekhriniso, through her clients, proudly informed all her friends and leaders of various ranks in the city and region about this. And the school director even helped Salima stay in the capital with her relatives. They accepted Salima as their own. In their house, the relatives were preparing for their son's wedding, and their new guest began to study the process with curiosity… Especially the 'pre-wedding rituals'.

She saw how the reciter of the Koran, the Bibi-Khalifa, came every day and conducted ritual events. Salima observed similar women's gatherings in her town, but unlike in Dushanbe, it was not customary to shower the reader with expensive gifts and large sums of money. And Salima realized, that in the capital, being the Bibi-Khalifa was a highly paid profession, and there was no need to study at universities to do it. These thoughts distracted the girl from concentrating on preparing for the exams and, of course, she 'successfully' failed them. She didn't want to return home, but also didn't know how she would live in Dushanbe.

On the wedding day of the owner's son, a tearful Salima sat by the ditch in the courtyard of the house. The sound of the karnay and surnay pipes had already begun ringing out – the bride and groom had arrived. They were surrounded by friends and family. Salima wiped away her tears and envied the participants in the celebration. Suddenly, she felt the gaze of the groom's friend on her, a handsome young man. He smiled sweetly at the stranger. Out of embarrassment, Salima jumped up and hurried to leave, but the man caught up with her. He sympathetically began to ask why such a wonderful girl was upset and alone. And Salima, surprising even herself, told him about her failure to enter the university. And how she doesn't know how to return home and look in her mother's eyes without guilt.

"Come on now, it's not the end of the world," the man began to reassure Salima. "You can enrol in preparatory courses or go to work to gain experience. And next year, be sure to go to university."

"Thank you for your kind words," Salima replied.

"What's your name, if it's not a secret?"

"Salima."

"Let's get acquainted, I'm Abdullo. Come with me - we'll go for a walk together at my friend's wedding."

"Oh, but it will be awkward! I'm only staying here because of my university exams."

"Well, that's alright! How about you be my girlfriend for the wedding? How does that sound?"

Salima agreed, deciding to forget about the hardships at least for a while. And she liked the gallant Abdullo.

When the dancing began, Abdullo invited her. Salima gracefully raised her hands and easily fluttered into the circle. Abdullo was about to join her, when the rest of the dancers suddenly paused and moved aside for Salima. Everyone was delighted and in awe of Salima's plasticity, her charming facial expressions, and graceful movements. She felt the music and conveyed the mood in the dance. Abdullo was surprised and subdued.

When the dance ended, there was thunderous applause. Salima was surrounded and compliments came from all sides. Abdullo even felt jealous and, pushing through her fans, stood in front of Salima:

"Wow! You dance so beautifully!"

"Wait until you hear me sing!" Salima answered smiling.

"So, sing, please!"

Salima shrugged her shoulders coquettishly, and Abdullo rushed to the presenter. They talked a bit about something and Abdullo, as a friend and witness to the groom, introduced Salima to the guests.

In a clear and ringing voice, she brought out the popular classical song from 'Shashmakom', and the musicians began to accompany her with feeling. And once again, there were exclamations of admiration around Salima for her talents.

That evening Abdullo fell in love. And he never left his Salima again. A month after their first meeting, they decided to get married. Abdullo was from Khujand, but when telling her stories, grandmother Salima did not like to remember his parents and relatives, she only insisted on the help of her mother Mekhriniso.

Having learned that Salima's mother was alone in Penjikent, Abdullo decided to transport her to Dushanbe. Mekhriniso sold her house, collected only essentials and moved in with the newlyweds. She did not get to rejoice at her daughter's happiness for long: in the winter, doctors discovered that she had an advanced form of tuberculosis. And soon, Mekhriniso died.

Even from the very beginning, Abdullo Qurboni's career was going as well as it possibly could. He graduated studying higher political courses in Moscow, defended his dissertation and lead the Republican Knowledge Society.

Salima had no time to think about studying at a university: she immediately became pregnant, gave birth to three children in a row, and plunged headlong into household chores.

I couldn't find out when and where Salima learned to read the Koran, but she quickly gained popularity in her circles and was often invited to women's ritual gatherings. Grandmother Salima did not teach any of her grandchildren to read suras from the Koran. She explained it simply:

"I don't want competition and I don't intend to share my bread with anyone."

Abdullo, after working in the Knowledge Society, was transferred to the Central Committee  government then became director of the Institute of Political History until the end of his career. He was a respected man, a doctor of historical sciences.

Salima became a powerful and proud woman. She raised two daughters just like herself. Mairam – who taught at the Pedagogical Institute, didn't marry for quite a long time, and her mother eventually forced her to marry a relative of the deputy director of a meat processing plant. They didn't have children for a long time. By the age of forty, Mairam had a daughter, Shokhina.

Sairam, through connections, graduated from the Institute of Arts, and after graduation she worked in a museum. She was also married, but to a promising chemist. And it happened like this: our grandmother performed a traditional ceremony in the rich house of the parents of her future son-in-law. And there, they asked her about their neighbour Sadbarg, whom they liked. But Salima immediately turned the conversation to her daughter Sairam, describing her wonderful qualities. And things worked out well. And the young couple got married.

The son-in-law was not handsome - he was bald, wore glasses and looked older than his years. Sairam then snorted more than once:

"I wanted a husband as handsome as brother Nariman! But instead, I have to live with the 'great scientist' and admire his bald head."

Both sisters could not stand their husbands and envied Sadbarg, because her sister-in-law was valued and respected at work, loved by both adults and children.

Shokhina, Mairam's daughter, was called nothing less than 'Shahinya' (the wife of a ruler). She was arrogant, domineering and unrestrained. She studied in the same class as my future bride Gulbahor and left unflattering memories of herself among her classmates. A conversation at a parent meeting in the ninth grade, where parents and children were invited, became the talk of the town.

When it came time for Shokhina's progress, the class teacher turned to her mother:

"Mairam Abdulloevna, you are also a graduate of our school, you know what our requirements are. Try to convince Shokhina that she shouldn't be so careless about her studies. She's not doing well in any of her subjects!"

But Mairam, without listening to the end, interrupted:

"Muallimah, don't worry! She will graduate from school as a good student, just like me. You told my mother the same thing about me. But, as you can see, I turned out fine. The main thing for a woman is not education, but luck. If she marries successfully and her husband carries her in his arms, then that's it, there is no greater happiness! We should strive for something like this."

"How can you say such a thing? You're not in a women's club, you're at school," the teacher tried to stop Mairam.

"Why not?" Mairam objected with a grin. "Some become astronauts, and others must raise the astronauts."

"Do you think that you are raising an astronaut like Tereshkova?"

"I am raising a real woman who will be the happiest she can be."

All the parents began to object indignantly, but Mairam took her daughter by the hand with a grin and left the parent meeting.

Sairam had a son and daughter - Romin and Simin. They were slightly older than Khovar and Anvar. But we didn't communicate with any of our aunts' children. Grandmother Salima called us, her grandchildren, 'kishlachnye' (country-folk), both to our face and behind our backs, never inviting us to stay either in her house or in the families of her daughters. But our father Nariman did not insist on meeting with his Dushanbe relatives. Either he was embarrassed by us, or he didn't want Zarnisor's eyes and ears prying into his family. Who knows?

Grandmother Salima managed to provide herself with a good life even without a higher education. Times had changed, foundations collapsed. The slogan of the 1917 revolution: "Religion is the opium of the people," was completely forgotten decades later; moreover, it turned out that faith can unite people in the republic. Both politicians and non-politicians 'turned' to God overnight.

Salima quickly realized that ritual events are a very expensive 'product.' She began to learn suras from the Koran and parables. She started a notebook and wrote everything down in Cyrillic. Samizdat books with verses and surahs from the holy book appeared in the markets, and Salima constantly bought them. Then the book, 'Folklore of the Tajik People', was published, which described in detail all kinds of traditions and rituals, and so Salima mastered the 'science' of becoming a 'reader of the people.'

Once my grandmother came to us in Zarnisor for her beloved son Nariman's birthday. The younger grandchildren began to read poetry, and Nilufar read from Jami's favourite:

*Bo dandon rachna dar fulod zadan,*
*Bo nohun rah dar horo buridan*
*Furu raftan ba otashdon nagunsor,*
*Ba pilki dida otashpora chidan.*
*Ba farki sar binhoda sad shutur bor,*
*Zee Maghrib chonibi Mashriq Davidan,*
*Basho bar Chomi osontar namoyad,*
*Ki bori minnati dunon kashidan.*

*Hardened steel, would chew through with teeth,*
*A path through granite, would scratch with nails,*
*Would dive face-first into the burning fiery hearth,*
*Would give up lashes to the heat, like burning tails,*
*Would carry weight from a hundred camels' backs,*
*Would measure east to west, across winding trails*
*For all these things would be much easier for Jami*
*Than bowing to sly scoundrels and their tall-tales.*

Everyone applauded, and Salima's grandmother grinned unkindly: "You learn poetry, you read different books - that's good. You will, like your mother Sadbarg, 'plough-away', day and night, and get pennies in return. I earn as much in one day as she would dream to earn in a month.

"Grandma, why don't you teach us your craft?" Nilufar asked naively.

"Nobody taught me. I did everything myself," Salima answered her grandchildren with pride.

Sadbarg's apartment, inherited from her father, was passed over to her mother-in-law after the wedding, although no one re-registered it. Salima boastfully emphasized that she now had the whole floor at her disposal. And that the daughter-in-law's apartment was her dowry, which now belonged to the Qurboni family.

"Sadbarg, do you think you've settled things with me?" She never got tired of reproaching her daughter-in-law. "There is no price in the world for the milk with which I fed Nariman and raised you such a husband."

Grandmother Salima did not hold back when talking about us either, her grandchildren, she constantly repeated that her son was the most handsome man the world had ever seen, and she constantly looked for flaws in her daughter-in-law. And my mother silently listened to her offensive words and endured. She knew that no amount of arguments would convince her mother-in-law. I was glad that we lived separately and away from our Dushanbe relatives. And that our mother's love was plenty!

Grandmother Salima lived a long life. She outlived her daughter-in-law Sadbarg. But when she learned about her beloved son Nariman's stroke, she fell ill. Her daughters did not want to care for their sick mother and brought her to Nariman, despite his stroke. They told us of their mother's last request - to be buried in Zarnisor. Anvar began sending money for a nurse, doctors and medicine. After three months of serious illness, our grandmother passed away. We, the three brothers, took all the troubles of burial and commemoration upon ourselves. They buried her next to Sadbarg, Nilufar and Aunt Parvin. Our father, Nariman, asked to leave a place between the graves of Sadbarg and Nilufar.

During my childhood years, I had observed that in many traditional families, daughters-in-law are looked upon with disdain. They are obliged to earn the 'cost of the mother's milk' which fed their future husbands in infancy. The mothers-in-law always force their daughters-in-law to do the most difficult work and are constantly looking for a reason to reproach them. This, of course, is not true in all families. But in most cases, such an attitude towards young and inexperienced women leads to tragedy. Daughters-in-law cannot withstand the oppression, bullying and domestic violence. They find only one way out - to commit suicide. Our beloved sister Nilufar also committed such a terrible act.

Mother held back and tried not to tell us, her children, about her relationship with her grandmother. She always repeated:

"There is a God above each of our heads. He is merciful and reasonable. He gives each of us tests. These trials make us stronger."

Mother's difficult life and grandmother Salima's dislike for her was always clear to us. I realized that my father made many of his mistakes under the influence of her negative attitude. But how could he not realize that he himself would suffer from this? After all, he could lose everything in the end.

And that is exactly what happened.

## CHAPTER NINE:

# Father Nariman

"My word is law!" is what my father liked to say a lot. Since childhood, I shuddered when I heard this phrase. Father kept everyone submissive and only allowed us to walk behind his back, not next to him. He didn't let anyone in his family get close and instilled fear with a glance. When he was at home, everyone felt uncomfortable. Between ourselves, we called him 'Kani Himcha?' meaning, "where is my stick?" We called him that because of the way he punished us for offending him. He would tear off a thick stem from a privet, strip it of its leaves, and give us a 'good' whip with the stick. This happened rarely, but reliably. Fortunately, father worked a lot and only came home late in the evening, so it was bearable.

When our sister Nilufar was born, father Nariman seemed to soften. He occasionally took her in his arms, and her mother quietly rejoiced that her daughter awakened good feelings in him. But the baby grew up and her father's stern gaze also rested on her, and a formal tone appeared in their conversations.

For a long-time I could not understand why dad was called Akhriman behind his back. It turns out that people knew more about him on the street than we did at home. The people within our circle loved my mother very much and did not say anything in front of her. She didn't know much about her husband's deeds, and if she did figure something out, she pretended not to know, and never reacted. I don't even remember my mother ever being jealous of my father. One morning I saw her crying, but with a smile, she said that soapy water had got in her eyes when she was washing her face.

Our father, Nariman, according to my grandmother, was the family's favourite. She indulged him in everything. His older sister Mairam was jealous of how she treated him and so tried to torment him, chasing her brother around, nagging him. But his parents loved Nariman for his kindness, diligence in his studies and his quick-wit. The head of the family, Abdullo Qurboni, was proud of his son and had high hopes for him. In the mornings, they would go for a run together, and in their free time they sat at the chessboard, read and discussed books.

But his mother Salima only called her son 'my Emir'. She praised him and said that he was the most noble and beautiful, and that none of those around him could compare with him. At home, she did not allow Nariman to do hard work and would call the neighbours' boys for help who ended up giggling behind the back of their white-handed peer. Abdullo tried to reason with his wife so that she would not raise her son to be spoiled and weak. He tried to get Nariman to do household chores: occasionally they worked together in the yard under the groans and sighs of Salima.

Of all the children, I observed the relationship between my parents the most and could not understand why my father decided to marry my mother. I never noticed any looks, actions or even the slightest bit of affection for his wife in any of their conversations. That was because he was not a husband, but her master, her owner!

I remember one time, my parents were invited to the wedding of my cousin Simin, whom Aunt Sairam called 'incomparable.' Father Nariman was already in the capital in the morning, and my mother and I decided to go from Zarnisor together. I cut and tied together a huge bouquet of white lilies. Mother smiled sadly and complained that our Nilufar would not be at the wedding - her mother-in-law would not let her come.

At the wedding venue in Dushanbe, there was no one to meet us as we went into the banquet hall. Mother and I headed to our table, which should have been on the raised platform where my father was, cheerful and flushed from drinking. But before we could get there, we were stopped by Aunt Sairam, who had suddenly appeared: she showed us to a table right next to the door and seated us with strangers. Mother wanted to leave the wedding, but she looked at me and resigned herself.

"There," Aunt Sairam said loudly, pointing to the front table, "those are places reserved only for members of the Qurboni family!"

"For God's sake," my mother answered calmly. "You are the only Qurboni in 'your' family, whereas there are six in ours.

"Aunt Sairam, why aren't we at the same table as dad?" I asked in surprise.

"Because I am the hostess of the wedding and decide who gets to sit where."

“Okay then, I’ll ask him myself,” I objected and headed to the main table.

Father saw me and asked why his son was alone. I replied that Aunt Sairam wouldn’t let my mother see him. Father laughed and ordered me to bring his other half.

When we reached the platform, Aunt Mairam was there, seated with her friends and their husbands in a circle. There seemed to be only one free chair left, and I told my mother to sit there, saying that I would be nearby with Cousin Romin and his friends.

“Okay, Ozar.”

The music started playing and I asked my mother to dance. She was shy, but I insisted.

“It’s good that you took me away from the table,” my mother whispered to me. “I sat there with the Qurboni family, like a stranger. No one paid me any attention, everyone was busy with their conversations.”

“We’ll dance, then we’ll tell father that we’ll be sitting down together. There should be a place at his table,” I reassured my mother.

Soon exclamations of admiration were heard around us - my mother danced very beautifully and tenderly. Some guests and her former students began to approach from all sides of the hall and loudly applaud.

Suddenly, the drunken aunts, Mairam and Sairam, appeared nearby and began to dance so vulgarly that my mother blushed. We went to my father. He didn't notice us and was talking to one of Aunt Sairam's cheerful friends with a playful expression on his face. Her husband was not at the table. Suddenly, my mother turned sharply and pulled me along with her to the exit of the hall.

I did not understand what was happening.

"I want to go home, Ozar. Let's leave!"

"But I have to warn father. You know how he is."

"It'd be better if you didn't go."

"I don't understand what happened?"

"It's okay, my dear, everything is fine."

Then Aunt Mairam ran up and, smiling sarcastically, asked:

"Where are you going?"

"We have a long way to go, so we decided to leave early,"

Mother answered.

"It seems to me that you are upset about something?" My aunt asked with feigned concern.

But she was interrupted by my mother's former students. Having surrounded their muallima (female teacher), they began to ask about her health, and recalled her lessons with great respect. The aunt turned away and left. Apparently, she didn't like these conversations.

Mother perked up but said that the wedding was noisy and that it would be better for them to meet her in Zarnisor in our yard to talk and reminisce about their school days. The students persuaded her to sit with them for at least a few minutes.

I went to tell my father that we were leaving. And he couldn't believe his ears: he was sitting down, surrounded by women who were openly clinging to him. And both my aunts, laughing loudly, counted out loud how long their brother Nariman kissed each one. I felt uneasy. I turned away and hurried to my mother. We left...

On the way home, I quietly stroked my mother's hand, thinking about how offensive my father's wild behaviour was to her. I was surprised that even in such difficult moments she felt sorry not for herself, but for me. She was worried that I would publicly condemn my father for obscenity.

We did not discuss what we saw at the wedding. "The sword of vengeance can cut you too," I mentally remembered the Eastern proverb and sighed involuntarily. And my mother, as if guessing my thoughts, sadly said:

"He who offends people will bring the same amount of offense to his children, to everyone he loves. A boomerang always returns to the one who threw it..."

And it's true. Simin's family life did not even last a single year - her husband left her. The father-in-law and mother-in-law did not even let their daughter-in-law stay in their house and Simin had to return to her parents. At two years old, Simin's first child was diagnosed with autism. My cousin began dating a married man with many children. She ruined his life, and when he was left without money, she left him. When I heard about it, I remembered my mother's prophetic words about the boomerang.

After what happened at the wedding, I still asked my father why he humiliated my mother with his behaviour. He looked at me sharply, as if surprised at the courage of such an 'interrogation,' and grinned smugly:

"I was drunk, so those women hung onto me. Although they would probably still chase after me even if I was sober. Listen, I am a man! I need attention and affection, but your mother is too cold, like the winter winds."

"Doesn't mother need attention, affection and tenderness?" I objected. "But when you're with her, you are always insensitive and rude. What kind of woman would stand something like that? There is a good proverb for this: 'You can't clap with only one hand.'"

"When did you become a professor at the Department of Language and Literature?" Father asked sarcastically. "You dare to try and teach me? I'm not your student! And I don't intend to take your tests in front of you, understand?"

And he left in anger, slamming the door. And I shuddered, thinking that he might take his anger out on my mother.

At home he could shut our mouths, but the deceived husbands did not remain silent. Rumours about the 'immoral women' around my father reached the top management and they stopped promoting my father, and trust in him was shaken.

But my father believed that all was not lost and continued to 'waste his life.' Women stuck to him like flies as long as he had money. But when they realized that Nariman was no longer useful, they abandoned him. My father wasn't used to this. He thought they loved him because he was handsome and fit. But there were many such 'Don Juans' around, and even younger and richer ones, so priorities changed.

Over the years, my father became increasingly tough and unpredictable. Nervousness and constant drunkenness erased the former attractiveness from his face. His foppishness and gallantry had disappeared. Even my father's proud gait changed; it seemed that he became shorter. He, of course, blamed his wife for his failures. I realized that my father loved no-one but himself. And he even managed to shut Salima up with money from time to time. He sometimes listened to his sisters and willingly participated in their intrigues. At the same time, he considered all women not as humans, but as a different species. Where did he get this mentality from? Was it because of how easily he 'used' them? Was it from his constant binges on the side and his permissiveness? Though most likely, it was thanks to his grandmother, she who buried a worm of narcissism into his body that settled in his soul and constantly ate away at him...

The death of his wife, Sadbarg, reminded him that not everything under the sun remains forever. However, on the fortieth day after my mother's wake, my father brought home a new wife – an imposing and self-confident young woman called Nazrimo. I stopped going home. The new 'mistress' behaved inappropriately: she either looked at me suggestively, or tried to hug me 'in a kindred way.'

Nazrimo quickly managed to give our father a stroke, taking all the valuables from the house and leaving her sick husband all alone. I don't know how long my father lay in this condition. Feeling something was wrong, I called home all day, but no one answered. I rushed home in a taxi and when I arrived, I reeled in horror: father was lying on the floor naked by the bed, all blue. I called an ambulance and took him to the hospital. Grandmother Salima, having learned about this, fell ill.

Father Nariman was kept hooked to machines for two weeks, and when he felt a little better, he asked to go home. He returned completely different. Our faithful neighbour Anora-kayvonu told me that when she came to visit our father, she almost did not recognize him – he was aged, with dull, helpless eyes. The left side of his face remained motionless, and our father could barely utter any words.

Aunts Mairam and Sairam immediately brought their sick grandmother Salima to our house. They explained to me that in Dushanbe there was no one to look after her, everyone was at work. They also conveyed our grandmother's last wish - to be buried in Zarnisor next to her son Nariman, despite the fact there was still a place for her next to the grave of her husband, Abdullo Qurboni, at the Dushanbe cemetery. They placed Grandma Salima in my mother's bedroom and she talked with her son Nariman through the open door. Her legs gave out and she had to live with her illness in a wheelchair. I could not leave my job in Dushanbe and my students at the university. I consulted with my brothers on the phone, and we decided to hire a nurse to look after my father and grandmother. Anvar sent money for a nurse, medicine, and a massage therapist.

But nothing helped grandmother Salima - she died quietly in her sleep. I had to take care of the funeral affairs. It was painful to look at my father: he could not even go to the cemetery, and when he finally did go to see the coffin, he uttered only two phrases:

"Forgive me, mother! Soon I will leave for you too..."

Grandmother was buried next to Nilufar. Aunts Mairam and Sairam saw their mother off on her last journey and left. They were offended that, in her will, she left all her property to her three grandchildren - Khovar, Anvar and Ozar.

After grandmother Salima passed away, father Nariman seemed to have lost himself. He lay with his face to the wall and did not say a word. The nurse despaired at attempting to get him out of this state and told me when we met that the patient needed a family: children and grandchildren would breathe life into the empty house. Doctors confirmed that our father was unlikely to survive another six months.

I wrote to my brothers. At first they didn't want to come, but then they decided to forgive our father. We all arrived with our families at the beginning of summer. Khovar and Vera's were free since the school holidays had begun, and their son Daniyar, with his red, curly hair, resembled our dear Nilufar, was happy to be in Zarnisor. Daniyar immediately informed his grandfather Nariman that in Gatchina his classmates called him Danila in Russian, and that his desk partner Sveta affectionately called him Danilka. And that his mother, Vera, will soon have another baby, but he does not yet know if it will be a brother or sister.

Anvar and Zarrina's children – their daughter, Makhbuba, and baby son, Mukhsinm – were not afraid of their sick grandfather, and came up to the bed to hug him. And when he cried with joy, Makhbuba took out an embroidered scarf from the pocket of her dress and began to wipe the tears from her grandfather's face, whispering tender, soothing words. I had a lump stuck in my throat from excitement and joy.

Our house has come to life. Zarrina and Vera were busy in the kitchen, preparing delicious and healthy dishes, Anvar and Khovar helped wash and change their father's clothes, smoothing out the awkwardness of these procedures with jokes, which were painful for his pride. One by one they took him out in a wheelchair into the garden and talked about something. The grandchildren rushed to their grandfather with drawings, asked him to answer various questions, sang and danced in front of him. Daniyar-Danilka dashingly danced 'Kalinka' with a stomp-slap and squat, and Makhbuba, to the sounds of the popular pop song 'Hey, Sanam!', gracefully twirling like an oriental princess. At night, the eldest grandson, Daniyar, would read fairy tales to his grandfather with a very serious face.

"This is happiness," our father repeated with tears in his eyes.

One morning he woke up early and said that he had a dream: our mother asked him to hold a family holiday and invite my fiancée Gulbahor. We happily began organizing the feast. My beloved's parents came from Dushanbe and met everyone. We invited neighbours and mother's colleagues from school, and Aunt Anora pleased everyone with her delicious dishes. For the first time in so many years there was music in the house. My father began to constantly remember his Sadbarg.

"Your mother was the best! Why didn't I try to save her?" He repeated sadly.

How could we answer that question for him?

Khovar and Anwar's holidays were over, they could not stay longer. But the daughters-in-law and their children decided to stay with us until the end of the summer.

Father became very friendly with Vera. She did not even remember that first meeting, when our father openly spoke out against Khovar's marriage. Now the father-in-law and daughter-in-law had heartfelt conversations for hours. One day I sat down next to Vera at my father's bed. He thanked me with a glance, wanting me to hear his revelations.

"Vera, you are a very kind, noble and merciful person. Tell me, can God forgive me? After all, according to his holy words, I am a great sinner. They said that I was a bad husband and a mediocre father. But a wonderful lover. So does that mean I am drowning neck-deep in the swamp of sin?" Asked the father. Vera gently massaged her father's inactive left hand and tried to console him:

"The biggest sin is one that you are not afraid to commit, it is when you are not afraid of heavenly punishment. Though you have already come to repentance, which means you have realized the unrighteousness of life. We must pray and ask God and people around us for forgiveness. All those who were offended and ruined by you, living and dead. Prayer is the cry of our soul, and it will be heard by everyone for whom it is intended, I believe in it."

"And I would like to believe in it as well... My beloved Sadbarg, my dear blood Nilufar - they are victims of my cruel temper, oppression and violence," the father answered with tears and trembling in his voice. "I am very guilty before them and before my sons. The only thing I ask of God is that he allows me to meet my loved ones in heaven."

"You will definitely meet them. They see everything from above and have long since forgiven you."

"Well, have you forgiven me?"

"The main thing is that God forgives. We are all human beings - sinners. And your sons are wonderful! They didn't leave you. This is all thanks to their mother, Sadbarg's, upbringing. I will never forget her beautiful soul, filled with love."

"Ozar," my father turned to me, "I know that you are the most important witness of my unworthy actions towards your mother Sadbarg. I look back on my life now and don't understand how I became such a monster. My father, Abdullo Qurboni, with his nobility, generosity and love of life has always been an example for me. I loved and tried to be the same as him. They say a son looks for a wife who behaves like his mother. But I didn't want this! My mother Salima, who was powerful and proud, henpecked my father. And he, it seems, secretly aware of this, chose the best of the best as my wife whilst already on his deathbed - the educated, bright, merciful Sadbarg. She brought joy, love and forgiveness to our family home. Which then dissolved in you four children. I didn't appreciate it. I knew that my mother and sisters tyrannized Sadbarg because they could not forgive her for the wonderful human qualities that they did not have. And I, myself, committed unworthy acts..."

My father cried, and Vera and I sincerely pitied and consoled him in this bitter repentance. Gulbahor also helped us, often coming to look after my father, helping Vera and Zarrina.

At the very end of summer, my father began to weaken. Doctors also confirmed that his life was fading. I called my brothers. Father Nariman asked to be buried between his wife Sadbarg and his daughter Nilufar. He said that the house he built here in Zarnisor did not become a place of unification and love. And he expressed the hope of seeing his family in a heavenly home - in another world.

We were struck by my father's last words:

"Now I understand why people called me Akhriman... It was for all the evil, grief and sadness I brought into this world. But I repent. Forgive me, my dear Khovar, Anvar and Ozar. It won't be easy for me in the next world. I apologize to you too, my dear daughters-in-law and grandchildren. And you, Ozar, for myself and for my mother, I bless you and Gulbahor."

Of course, this was a late repentance. But we let him go in peace...

Now our father is forever united with his wife and daughter, and nearby are the graves of Aunt Parvin and Grandmother Salima. We, the sons, fenced off this place. It turned out to be a family crypt. Maybe my father's soul will find peace there...

## CHAPTER TEN:

# Gulbahor

The brightest chapter of my book is dedicated to you, my Gulbahor. Fate led us to our joyous encounter with one another, and now we have been building our family together for several years. We have two wonderful sons, Farzon and Tabriz, whom their friends jokingly call Tarzan and Tarbuz (watermelon). Our long-awaited daughter, Sadbarg, was recently born - she was named after my mother.

But I remember that once, I was even afraid to introduce you to my parents. I didn't want you to know about our family problems. We met in Dushanbe, at the university, where I became a teacher. Already as a graduate student, I began giving lectures at the Faculty of Philology and from the very first classes I felt that some of interest the female students had in me was not at all scientific. Their intrusive attention was unpleasant, and I carefully averted my gaze from the girls' faces.

But you, Gulbahor, were completely different – you were serious, inquisitive and very beautiful. You didn't emphasize your natural beauty in any way, you didn't care about looking super fashionable and defiantly attractive like your classmates. But your wide eyes and sweet smile did not give me peace during lectures nor at home.

I entered the classroom, quickly greeted the students, and my gaze instantly found you, Gulbahor. My heart melted with your joyful silent response: I saw the reciprocal emotions in your sweet face. Your sensitivity was astounding, although I hid my worries about domestic troubles. You often came up to me after lectures with a trivial question just to look into my face or stand next to me for at least a minute. You were not at all like my mother Sadbarg and sister Nilufar – I did not feel resignation and slavish obedience in your character. It seemed to me that you were a dream girl with the wonderful name, Gulbahor, which means spring flower. You were positive, sincere, purposeful, open, proactive and correct. In the symphony of our glances, currents of tenderness, love and your endless faith in me flowed from your soul. I felt that a man had awakened in me, capable of loving this girl. I understood that Gulbahor would be my eternal spring, but I did not immediately decide to confess my love.

This happened after the successful defence of your thesis. On the recommendation of the faculty academic council, you were accepted into graduate school, and I, at your request, was approved as a scientific supervisor. I invited you to celebrate this event together with me in a new cafe in the central city park. We talked about a lot of things, but I made the main confession when you, understanding my embarrassment, hugged me around the neck and trustingly laid your head on my shoulder. I held you to my chest with trepidation and whispered:

“My dear, I fell in love with you from our first meeting. I couldn’t imagine being apart from you for more than a day and I dream of eventually uniting our destinies. And you, Gulbahor? Do I dare ask if you feel the same way?"

You looked into my eyes and answered without affectation:

"I've been waiting for your confession for a long time, Ozar! Thank you for this happy moment. I also love you very much and want us to be together."

"We need to go to Zarnisor and meet my mother. I can imagine how happy she will be to see my chosen love. It's just a pity that my mother is sick and can't recover from the untimely death of my sister Nilufar."

"Let's not rush to meet our parents. My friends had already told me about Ozar Qurboni's mother; she also spoke at the defence of your dissertation. And I also heard something about Nilufar, who passed away at a very young age... I would like to know everything about you and your family."

"These are very sad stories. I'll definitely tell you. But from now on, shouldn't we address each other less formally?"

"Sure, that sounds good to me!"

We didn't have time to go to Zarnisor and you, Gulbahor, never saw my mother. Only after her funeral did I tell you about the tragedy with Nilufar and my father's cruel attitude towards us.

How different our family was from yours! You lovingly told me that your father Huseynov Akmal is the director of the republican public library, and your mother Dilorom Ikrami is a famous paediatrician at the central clinical hospital. You yourself are interested in tennis, music, psychology, and you have complete trust and mutual understanding with your parents.

I remember when I inquired about the topic of your future dissertation and was very confused when I heard your answer:

“I want, based on materials from fiction and journalism, to explore the topic of domestic violence in Tajikistan.”

“Why did you choose such a complex and almost unsolvable problem?”

“Because this problem is hushed up even in so-called intelligent and modern families. Here’s just one example: I had a classmate, Zumrad Raufova, who was from a simple working-class family with many children. She was smart, beautiful, kind, sympathetic, an activist and a favourite of the class. Several classmates were in love with her at once.

But my friend was married off early to a well-known family in the republic, and it turned out that the groom had a woman and a child in Moscow, where he completed his studies. All this was kept secret for the time being. Zumrad didn’t know anything. Her husband constantly went on business trips. Then he would stay in Moscow for a long time. My friend gave birth to a daughter. And, without warning anyone, she went to see her husband. There the truth was revealed. The husband abandoned both Zumrad and their daughter.

Zumrad returned to Dushanbe, and instead of support and help from her loved ones, she heard only words of reproach and condemnation. She didn't live long in the hostel because her husband's parents didn't want to help her, they pointed to the front door and told her to leave, and she was ashamed to return to her family's house. Out of despair, Zumrad and her daughter jumped off a bridge. She didn't tell anyone anything; everything happened unexpectedly for many of us. And for me too. I still don't believe it."

"This story is unfortunately very familiar to me," I said, taking a deep breath. "It is difficult and sometimes impossible to fight this in our imperfect society."

"I agree. People shouldn't be left alone with their problems to withdraw into themselves. There is no need to be afraid of anything - neither words of condemnation, nor conversations of ill-wishers, nor the occasional biased public opinion. If Zumrad had told me, I would not have left her alone. There are no hopeless situations. How can someone take their own life like that? Why are the parents indifferent to their daughters who are in trouble? Why don't their brothers and sisters, who know and see everything, protect them?"

I was silent. I was ashamed of my inaction regarding Nilufar. I thought, perhaps, my mother, with her kindness and resignation, instilled in us unforgivable obedience. We brothers were afraid of offending our mother and upsetting our capricious father. And this led to a terrible tragedy...

"If only I had known about Nilufar earlier! I saw how nervous you were, your eyes showed the pain of your soul. I wanted to help. But we weren't that close. And you were silent the whole time. There is a good proverb: "Ba guzashta salavot," meaning, "we only question the past."

"Before she passed away, my mother blamed herself very much for Nilufar's death. And today I scold myself for not helping either my sister or my mother. I can understand my mother, but I won't forgive myself," I lowered my head.

"This is what my future dissertation is about. We need to teach girls and young women how to defend themselves. We must try to improve society. Otherwise, you end up with two extremes - either constant tolerance of domestic violence, or suicide."

"But how can I guide your research if I myself could not resist domestic violence?"

"I really need you as a witness, because before your very eyes, a tragedy happened with your sister. Of course, we can't do this without consulting lawyers, psychologists and education system workers. But let's not talk about this anymore today. I see how I upset you. We have two years of work ahead of us on our dissertation."

We met every day and couldn't stop talking to each other. We stood outside your house for a long time. And one day I saw your mother waiting for us at the entrance. She smiled welcomingly and said:

"We finally meet, Ozar. Gulbahor has buzzed into everyone's ears, talking about you. She praised her chosen love so much, that my father and I fell in love with you in absentia."

Gulbahor, your cheeks turned red from embarrassment:

"Mother, there's no need to give away my secrets!"

"Let's invite Ozar to visit, then there will be no secrets," said Dilorom Khalimovna.

"I will discuss this with Ozar, Mummy!"

"Okay, I won't bother you," your mother agreed and, saying goodbye, went into the house.

"Gulbahor," I suggested, "I need to meet your father Akmal Khasanovich. I'll go to his library tomorrow for a men-to-man conversation. And then we can visit you at home."

"As you say Ozar. Bye then. Talk to you tomorrow? I'll be studying in the library if you need anything."

I walked around the city for a long time and thought about our conversation. I couldn't sleep at night. With you, Gulbahor, I became more confident and courageous. I realized that all human prejudices in us come from uncertainty and fear of public opinion. For every step taken, a person himself must answer to his conscience, to his loved ones and relatives. You are right, my Gulbahor.

The meeting with my future father-in-law went as if we had known each other for many years - relaxed and sincere. You, Gulbahor, led me to your father's office, and you hurried to the reading room. Akmal Khasanovich captivated me immediately: a man of few words, a good listener, an intelligent and serious person, with a great sense of humour.

"Yesterday I was surprised by my wife's joy: after your meeting, she chirped with me like a bird. Now I understand why, such a handsome young man will be next to our Gulbahor, and I'm also glad about it.

We talked for a long time, looking closely at each other. Akmal Khasanovich spoke slowly and academically correctly, but did not boast of being well-read, and behaved simply and very friendlily. I really liked it. I felt that we had a lot in common. And I also realized that he liked it too. "Well, how was your conversation?" you asked, entering your father's office.

"This is how I imagined your chosen one, my dear Gulichon," Akmal Khasanovich hugged both of us by the shoulders with a smile. "But there is a long road of life ahead, with ups and downs. Be prepared to overcome all obstacles and live with dignity. Now, I hope we will have a lot of time to talk. You can come to our home, Ozar, we will always be glad."

We said goodbye and decided to go for a walk along the middle alley of our capital. I saw how happy you were, Gulbahor, and tried to relieve your excitement with a joke.

"Why are you 'Qurboni?' Are you like a lamb waiting to be slaughtered, since the surname literally means 'sacrifice'. You know, our last name is Husseini! Hussein means handsome! Why don't you change to my surname? Wouldn't it suit you better?"

"My great-grandfather was born on the sacred holiday of Qurbon – on the day of sacrifice. Such children are considered happy and are named after the holiday. That's where our last name comes from," I answered smiling.

"I'm kidding, Ozar Qurboni! I just want to keep my last name. If you don't mind? Our dad has two daughters. My sister, Gulrukhsor, studies in Moscow. There are no sons in my family. Dad will be pleased if I continued his legacy."

"Of course, my dear."

I was struck by the aura in your house, Gulbahor. I have never seen anything like this in Zarnisor. Your parents, like doves, talked and cooed to each other quietly and tenderly. Your father helped your mother and sat down at the table when everything was ready for dinner. And I was naturally attracted to be an assistant. I have never seen such an ideal scene. My father, like my grandmother, always sat at the head of the table and gave orders to everyone, and we were all subordinate.

After a wonderful dinner, Akmal Khasanovich and I sat down at the tea table. He very delicately asked about my mother and Nilufar, which he listened to carefully. I couldn't tell him everything, but he didn't insist. From my stories, he liked my brothers Khovar and Anvar. I told him a little about my father. Akmal Khasanovich regretted that my sister and mother would not witness our happiness with Gulbahor. I was grateful to him for these words.

Time passed rapidly, we didn't even notice it. I realized that I had found a second family in this house.

After my mother died and my father had a stroke, I had to spend more time in Zarnisor. At work there were vacations and long summer holidays. My brothers and their families came when I called. The doctors warned us that father Nariman would get worse in autumn and that having his children and grandchildren around will give him the will to live a little longer.

We talked a lot about you, my Gulbahor, with my brothers Khovar and Anvar, with their wives Vera and Zarrina. Our father did not react at all. But the changes in his character pleased me. I still suffered through his lack of blessing for the wedding. But you helped me with this, Gulbahor. You came to our house yourself, met your future father-in-law, sat by his bed and somehow quietly called the patient for a sincere conversation. I was surprised to see a spark of interest in my father's eyes and his unusually shy smile.

You didn't try to look for his flaws with your gaze. Father Nariman held your hand and asked you not to leave, but to stay with us longer. He seemed interested in talking with you. Carefully and intelligently, you asked father Nariman many leading questions that tested him, but he gave the necessary answers. I was amazed by your interaction, because my father had never opened his soul to anyone like that.

And then one morning my father called me and told me that he had seen my mother in a dream: she asked him to meet the parents of my fiancée Gulbahor here in Zarnisor. I kissed my father's emaciated hand with pity and heard his repentant words:

"I want you to organize the engagement as quickly as possible. I don't have long to live. If your mother were alive, you wouldn't believe how happy she would be..."

My brothers and I went to your parents, Gulbahor, and we invited everyone to a common family celebration.

How happy we all were! My father, who before his illness could not recognize his children's own choices, now understood a lot. And I forgave him for everything.

After my father's death, after completing all the funeral rites, we got married. Before the wedding, I renovated the house with the help of my brothers, helped by interior designers and a gardener. And we cleaned and landscaped the garden and built a beautiful greenhouse on the site of Aunt Parvin's burnt house. We planted lemon trees and sadbarg roses there.

And another joy befell me - through mutual acquaintances, I found the son of Aunt Parvin and my childhood friend, Ravshan. He came to the wedding with his beautiful wife Nargis and son Parviz. Ravshan and I went to the cemetery to visit our relatives and pray for them. And Ravshan placed a bouquet of white lilies on Nilufar's grave. I realized that he had not forgotten his childhood love.

Nargis has become very friendly with you, Gulbahor, as well as with Vera and Zarrina. We talked about a lot during the week of their stay. And we decided to meet as families every year.

You, Gulbahor, fell in love with our town Zarnisor and called this place a land shining with gold. I decided that we would stay to live here so that Mother Sadbarg would rejoice from heaven.

"This is Saadi's 'Guliston' and 'Buston' combined. Guliston is a flower garden, Buston is a fruit garden. Saadi probably wrote his famous poetic and prose parables in a similar place," you repeated with admiration. An unforgettable event in our lives was the day you defended your dissertation, Gulbahor. There were many people there and many opponents who attacked your proposals to eradicate some ancient rituals and traditions.

"Our problem is that we just can't break out of the Middle Ages," you calmly retorted. "Everything in the world is changing, it's time to live in such a way as not to become slaves to thousand-year-old rituals. I propose to introduce a general education program and legal education. It's time to accept that men and women are equal. Patriarchy must disappear in our reality, and not be declared. You shouldn't hold lavish weddings and ritual events to surprise people, and then land the newlyweds with the costs. Why don't religious leaders explain to the groom's parents that according to the sacred scriptures, a daughter-in-law should be a good mother and raise worthy children and should not owe anything to the groom's parents. No one has the right to make her a slave. And a young daughter-in-law should not remain silent even at the slightest sign of oppression and violence. Everyone should know that she is not being treated according to the rules of law and morality. Targeted support from government and legal authorities is needed to normalize family relations in the republic and eradicate domestic violence. It is necessary to understand that public opinion is not always objective and due legal attention should be paid to each case. It is necessary to publicly condemn and punish those who are the perpetrators of domestic violence, especially incitement to suicide."

I am incredibly proud, Gulbahor, that you managed to tear down public opinion. Based on the materials of your dissertation, brochures and visual aids have been published in pedagogical universities, law enforcement organizations, ministries of education and health. They suggested using your research as the basis for a doctoral dissertation. And in Zarnisor you opened a Centre for Assistance and Rehabilitation for Victims of Domestic Violence.

We live in perfect harmony. In our family, the sons are the descendants of the Qurboni and Husseini families: I named our youngest son after my grandfather Akmal so that his legacy would continue. Your father and you, Gulbahor, even shed tears of happiness.

I often cut roses and lilies in the garden, I remember my mother, Nilufar and father Nariman. I look at the sky and hope for their reconciliation. And I also think, does my father see the happiness that has settled in his house?

*Moscow – London*

*2021*

www.ingramcontent.com/pod-product-compliance
Lightning Source LLC
Chambersburg PA
CBHW030602310726
48979CB00003B/539

* 9 7 8 1 9 1 3 3 5 6 7 3 6 *